Chinese American Intermarriage

Chinese American Intermarriage

By Betty Lee Sung

1990
Center for Migration Studies
New York

The Center for Migration Studies is an educational,
non-profit institute founded in New York in 1964
to encourage and facilitate the study of socio-demographic,
economic, political, historical, legislative and pastoral
aspects of human migration and refugee movements.
The opinions expressed in this work are those of the author.

Chinese American Intermarriage

First Edition
Copyright 1990 by
The Center for Migration Studies
All rights reserved. No part of this book may be reproduced
without permission from CMS.

CENTER FOR MIGRATION STUDIES
209 Flagg Place, Staten Island, New York 10304–1199

ISBN 0–934733–47–3   ISBN 0–934733–48–1 (paper)

Library of Congress Number: 90–xxxxx
Printed in the United States of America.

This Book is Dedicated
to All My Grandchildren
Present and Future

Contents

List of Tables

List of Figures

Acknowledgements

The gestation period of a book, beginning with the germination of an idea to publication in hand, is a lengthy one. In comparison to human birth, the striking difference is that the entire time with a book is given to hard labor and contractions that never let up until the work is born. Fortunately, the process can be facilitated when helping hands and encouraging words make the task a bit easier.

Special thanks goes to Tony Bernard. I relied upon Tony completely for all the statistical programming and tabulation of the data from the census and marriage license applications. Without Tony's computer expertise, I would have been stymied. A multiple amputee, Tony could still tap the computer keys faster than most people. Words cannot express my admiration for this man who fought and overcame every odd imaginable to earn a doctorate and become a highly respected member of the New York City government.

I was assisted in going through the 142,000 marriage license applications by three students from The City College of New York, who volunteered their time and effort. They were James Lum, Sonia Jung, and Siu Ying Ng. Siu Ying even designed the form for easier computer input. Eventually, Won Yee Tom joined this research effort which was laborious and time-consuming. Just think of these students' dedication in giving up their free time to help me go through dusty files in scattered marriage license bureaus of the five boroughs. Let me publicly thank them now, and when they see this book, I hope they feel rewarded for their efforts.

Mayor David N. Dinkins, then City Clerk in charge of the New York City Marriage License Bureau, gave me permission to access the files. His staff, in particular Mr. Joseph Sanfedele, was most cooperative and helpful. At that time, I was the second person ever given permission to view the applications, the first being Father Joseph Fitzpatrick, Professor Emeritus of Sociology at Fordham University. Father Fitzpatrick preceded me by doing research on intermarriage among Hispanics. He gave me much valuable advice and graciously read and edited the manuscript, recommending it for publication to Father Lydio Tomasi, Executive Director of the Center for Migration

Studies. At the Center, Mrs. Eileen Reiter edited the manuscript, greatly improving upon the prose. To all these people, I am most grateful.

To undertake the research, I was awarded two grants from the Research Foundation of the City University of New York. The panel of judges felt that my topic was timely and important. Their awards also signaled a trust in me to come through with a meaningful study. I hope I have fulfilled their expectations.

To all the interviewees who shared with me their experiences and insights into intermarriage, I owe the greatest debt of gratitude. I promised you anonymity, so I cannot reveal your names. I disguised your identity by giving you fictitious names. You may recognize your own words and your own experiences, but I am sure they are not recognizable by others. For those following or who contemplate following your footsteps, may they be guided by your experiences.

From the intermarriages of three of my children to date, I gained much insight. I presume more of my offspring will follow suit when they marry. The trend has been set in motion and is irreversible. We best learn as much as we can about this growing social phenomenon.

Betty Lee Sung

1

Introduction

Historically, all groups have opposed intermarriage. Preservation of group identity is almost instinctual, so social and legal sanctions against outmarriage have been strong and the consequences of defiance severe. Sons and daughters have been cast out of the family. Jewish families sit *shiva* or ritually mourn the newlywed as if he or she were dead. Society has considered unions between races mongrelization, and such intermarriages have been considered taboo or illegal. Children of the intermarried couple have suffered social ostracism and identity crises, often pulled between two groups but accepted by neither.

If sanctions are so strong, why is intermarriage seemingly on the rise? Are forces of which we are unaware operating to pull down the barriers, and what has triggered the mechanism of change? What follows in the wake of change, and how will the social fabric be altered? Answers to questions like these can come only from studying the phenomenon of intermarriage and the people involved, and that is the aim of this book.

There was a time when natural boundaries isolated races and nationalities. Oceans, mountains, rivers, sand or ice kept people separated for centuries. Legal barriers existed as well. Crossing from one country to another required passports, exit visas and entry visas. Transportation facilities determined access or egress as well. People who were isolated remained homogeneous in culture, language, outlook and physical characteristics. They married and reproduced among themselves. They rejected outsiders or subjected them to mistrust and suspicion.

However, with technological revolution, even the most remote tribe or village now can be reached by air within days if not hours. Television exposes us to different cultures. The telephone can put us in touch within seconds. Although some countries retain stringent regulations about entering or leaving the nation's borders, most are quite liberal. As a result, the human migration stream has reached epic proportions, especially within cities like New York, literally the crossroads of the globe. Cross fertilization is an inevitable by-product of the mobility and currents of human streams.

HOSTILE ATTITUDE

Technology may have catapulted us into the future, but cultural attitudes tend to lag behind. With the intermingling of races, men and women meet, become attracted to one another and wish to marry. Yet suspicion and mistrust of those not like ourselves remain. Even as society frowns upon mixed marriages, factors such as proximity, acculturation and the biological urge prevail. For example, the first Chinese man to come to the United States, Yung Wing, eventually married a white woman, Mary Louisa Kellogg (Lee, 1971). One of the first Chinese women on the American scene, Lalu Nathoy, became the wife of Charlie Bemis and came to be known as Polly Bemis (McCunn, 1981). Both marriages took place in the 1800s when the very thought of a marital partner across racial lines brought shock and fear to people's minds and sanctions against the union.

LEGAL SANCTIONS

The sanctions were both severe and strong. In many states, miscegenation laws prohibited and outlawed mixed marriages between Asians and whites. In states where it was declared illegal, interracial marriages were null and void. Children of the issue were illegitimate. The parties involved could be thrown into jail and/or fined. Even those who performed the ceremonies could be penalized (Murray, 1950). These miscegenation laws were not declared unconstitutional until 1967. In states where the law did not intervene, public sentiments were strong enough to discourage such unions.

Hostility was not just confined to the American public. As a matter of fact, the Chinese were no less adverse to intermarriage. Until recently, there were few Chinese females in this country. Chinese men in the United States invariably returned to China to seek brides, even though they knew that exclusion laws would prevent their wives from joining them here. Consequently, having a Chinese wife meant living a celibate life until the husband had earned enough money to return to China.

Miscegenation laws were not the only area of discrimination against the Chinese. In fact, Chinese were not even allowed into the United States after 1882. Those who remained could never become citizens. They could not vote. They could not testify in court. They could not own land. They were segregated from the larger society (Sung, 1967).

Not until 1943 did the doors open a crack to admit 105 Chinese persons per year. The doors did not fully open until 1965, when the laws were changed, and Chinese immigration has increased dramatically since. Where total Chinese population in the United States was but 78,000 in 1940, it is now more than a million and a half and growing rapidly. Each year, close to 50,000

Chinese enter the country as immigrants from China, Taiwan and Hong Kong (U.S. Immigration and Naturalization Service). Other Chinese come from Vietnam, Malaysia, Thailand, Cambodia, Burma and Laos as well as the Caribbean and Latin American countries. In addition, the immigrant category numbers are enhanced by refugee admissions. By the year 2000, the Population Reference Bureau of Washington predicts that Asians will make up 9.3 percent of New York City's population, the bulk of these numbers Chinese.

The tremendous increase in numbers has altered the size of the Chinese population, and the social climate has changed also. Chinese now have the right to become citizens. The Civil Rights Act of 1964, followed by Affirmative Action in 1972, set the stage for upward socioeconomic mobility. The ethnic movements of the 1960s and 1970s brought about better acceptance of and wider opportunities for minority peoples. New immigrants who come today are unlike the old. They possess skills and education. They come with the intention to stay, rather than merely to make money and return home. A new image, a new outlook and better acceptance laid the foundation for mingling and mutual attraction between the sexes from all ethnic groups. Conditions are now more conducive to intermarriage.

FAMILIAL CONCERNS

One of the biggest concerns of any ethnic group is loss of identity either through cultural or physical amalgamation. Intermarriage dilutes both. That is why it has always been frowned upon by the in-group as well as the out-group. When Chinese children date interracially, family relations become hostile and strained. When offspring intermarry, often the family rift never heals. Some parents disown their children and cut off all contact. The offspring suffer emotional anguish when their choice of a mate is rejected by the parents. As intermarriages increase, fissures and fractures within Chinese American families become more common, creating dissension, conflict and unhappiness.

PERSONAL CONCERNS

Parties to the intermarriages grope for direction and advice. Doubts abound, and they search for some ray of light to guide them in a venture that does not have much precedence. To what extent will their physical differences pose problems—not just to outsiders, but to themselves and their offspring? Are religious differences a potential source of trouble? What happens if cultural values do not mesh? How does one overcome family objection? Is lack of English fluency an obstacle to spousal communication? How does one cope with uncomplimentary remarks and hostile stares by outsiders? Do children of mixed unions encounter problems of marginality, never to be fully accepted by either group? Will they feel split within themselves? Will they suffer socially and psychologically?

SOCIETAL CONCERNS

Theories of migration have focused more on labor supply in response to economic conditions and less on the interaction of the migratory groups upon the host society in terms of human relations. In an open and mobile environment, intermarriage may be an inevitable by-product of migration. It can also be a measurement of social distance, assimilation, racial tolerance or cultural maintenance. Because objections tend to overshadow acceptance of mixed marriages, the negatives seem to outweigh the positives, but the latter should also be brought to light. Marital assimilation would be the ultimate degree of acceptance between majority and minority groups. When physical features are blurred through intermarriage, racial prejudice and discrimination may diminish and eventually disappear.

Infusion of new cultures and new blood has always resulted in the invigoration of a nation. As for offspring, a widespread perception is that children from mixed marriages are better looking, more intelligent and more creative. Is this fact or fiction?

NEED FOR STUDY

Because the discussion of intermarriage has been ruled more by emotions than by rational examination, and because there were few mixed marriages in the past, only a smattering of studies have been conducted on the subject. The Jews, more than any other group, have focused attention on what they consider a serious issue, therefore the literature primarily relates to Jews. A few studies have been done on other groups—Father Joseph Fitzpatrick and Douglas Gurak (1975) studied the Puerto Ricans and Hispanics in New York City; Andrew Lind (1967) and Romanzo Adams (1937) wrote on mixed marriages in Hawaii; Harry Kitano (1982) and John N. Tinker (1982) looked at intermarriage among Japanese Americans in Los Angeles, but the literature on intermarriage is sparse, especially that relating to the Chinese in this country. In 1951, Schwartz published an article on "Mate Selection among New York City's Chinese Males, 1931–1938" in the *American Journal of Sociology*. The data is half a century old. No study has been done in San Francisco, the city with the largest Chinese population in the country. The time is ripe for a look at intermarriage among the Chinese in New York City.

New York City is a metropolis like no other. The city is a magnet that draws upon a three-state surrounding area. It is a hub where people come together, circulate and pass through. It is said that there are more Jews in New York City than in Tel Aviv, more Irish than in Dublin, and more Puerto Ricans than in San Juan. No Tower of Babel could exceed the number of languages spoken by different ethnic groups throughout the city. Of course, this diversity leads to a more liberal and tolerant attitude toward people of different races and nationalities. Yet in spite of the variety and intermingling of peoples, ethnicity continues to be strong, particularly with groups who are recent immigrants.

METHODOLOGY

When the need for understanding of intermarriage is so great, it is surprising that so little research has been done on the subject, particularly with respect to the Chinese. A computer search of three major databases of social science indexes, including *Dissertation Abstracts*, came up with almost nothing. Statistics on the Chinese, unfortunately, are very limited and seldom collected or tabulated by governmental agencies. A study of intermarriage among Chinese Americans would involve basic and primary data collection procedures that are time consuming and tedious. This has been discouraging to researchers. But as we increasingly encounter an issue that is a marker of profound societal changes, the issue must be addressed.

This study is based upon data from intermarriages among the Chinese in New York City, although data from other places and other ethnic groups are introduced for comparative purposes. The reason for using New York City data is its large Chinese population, which numbered 150,000 in 1980, but which may exceed 300,000 in 1990. Much of the statistics came from marriage license applications that must be examined individually, as the law proscribes ethnic identification. Special permission was obtained for this inspection, and confidentiality had to be pledged. The size of the population of New York City can be equivalent to many a county, state or even some European nations. The number of applications examined in this study ran to 72,500 for 1972 and 69,100 for 1982, the two years used for the research. Moreover, each of the five boroughs comprising New York City had its own marriage license bureau. Since the data was scattered, the data collection task was rendered more time consuming and laborious.

Marriage licenses are the best source of information for marriages that are taking place or have taken place. The licenses usually reflect actual marriages. The applications supplied age, address, occupation, parents' names and birthplaces, and information on previous marriages, if any. Data from the licenses are limited. Ethnicity is not specified and was deduced only from surname, birthplace or birthplace of the parents. Chinese surnames are easily recognizable, especially to this researcher. Japanese, Vietnamese and Indian surnames are also readily identifiable as were Hispanic names. Jewish names were checked against a list of common Jewish surnames. It was impossible to delineate blacks from whites using surnames or place of birth.

Prior to the marriage license search, a special tabulation of the 1980 census for New York City was completed. That data source yielded a different set of information based upon total Chinese population residing in New York City. It reflected marriages contracted in China, in other states or anywhere at any time, as long as the participants were residents of New York City on census day in 1980. The census tabulation was based upon two Public Use Sample Tapes, the one percent and the five percent, for a six percent sample. The findings from that study have already been published (Chinese Historical Society, 1987). The research based upon findings from marriage license applications focuses on marriages currently taking place on American soil, which reflect the impact of migration and assimilation. In this study, census data may be used to augment license data, but only when such data is not obtainable from the licenses. It is important to differentiate between the two data sources, and statistics will always be identified by source—census or license.

Statistics from these two government sources provide numerical measurements and correlations, but they cannot answer questions on the quality of such marriages and the personal experiences of the couples involved. This information must be obtained by interviews with intermarried couples. Random sampling could not be employed. There is no known list or roster of Chinese intermarried couples, and a random sampling of the general population would be inefficient and not net enough cases to be meaningful. Therefore, the snowball sampling technique was employed.

Snowball sampling means using one respondent or interviewee to lead to others. Intermarried couples tend to associate with or be more aware of others like themselves. This sampling technique was found to be quite effective in locating respondents and interviewees. At the onset, with only a handful of leads to go by, there was a great deal of uncertainty as to how to identify mixed couples and how to contact them. The snowball technique worked well. Usually, an interviewee would suggest two or three others and even make the preliminary contacts to smooth the way for the interviewer. The goal was to interview fifty cases preferably with both husband and wife. In some instances, however, this was not feasible, due to divorce, separation or unwillingness to be interviewed. More husbands balked than wives. It was not an easy task getting people to talk about their intimate relationships, so if one partner kept refusing or ducking the interview, this researcher had to be content with one side of the story.

Each interview lasted about 45 to 90 minutes. The preferable method was to interview husband and wife separately and this practice was generally followed. In some instances, the couples indicated that "they had nothing to hide from each other" and wished to be interviewed together. In those cases, their wishes were respected. This writer conducted all of the interviews personally. The interviews were not structured, but a guideline was followed. Five general areas pertaining to intermarriage provided the framework for the questioning. They were: 1) Factors leading to the intermarriage; 2) Quality of spousal relationship; 3) Family reaction; 4) Societal attitude; and 5) Children of the union.

The purpose of the interviews was to obtain case studies of what actually happens when two people of different ethnic backgrounds unite in matrimony. Do differences in cultural upbringing or racial features cause problems beyond those inherent in all marriages? How did the couples deal with these issues, and were such coping mechanisms effective or ineffective? The interviews provided the incidents, the comments, the stories, the anecdotes, the human drama not obtainable from a purely statistical study. These are not extreme cases such as those cited by psychiatrists or social workers who deal with people encountering problems. They are ordinary couples in everyday life. Bias toward the positive may have resulted because some couples experiencing difficulties did not want to reveal their personal problems. However, among our cases, there were unsuccessful as well as successful examples.

Analysis of the data from the census and from marriage license applications, combined with direct interviews, reveals whether intermarriage is on the rise or decline (Chapter 2) and what the correlational factors are (Chapter 3). Chapter 4 looks at factors that draw a man and woman from widely separated ethnic backgrounds together in matrimony. Spousal relations and marital success and stability are discussed in Chapter 5, while the next chapter focuses on how the extended family reacts. The degree of societal acceptance or rejection is the topic of Chapter 7. Whether the children of such unions shoulder a heavier burden of confused identity or are beneficiaries of cross-fertilization physically and mentally is examined next. Finally, the last chapter explores the social implications and dynamics of change.

This book is a first attempt to look at the phenomenon of intermarriage among Chinese in New York City. It reveals the extent of marriages taking place between Chinese Americans and other ethnic groups. It throws light on the characteristics of these intermarrying couples, and puts into words the experiences and comments of a few who have traveled the road and can point out the pitfalls as well as the scenic spots on the highway of intermarriage.

2

Has a Trend Emerged?

In the mid-1970s, when the findings of a 30 percent rate from a study on Jewish intermarriage was presented, the response in the Jewish community was shock, horror and fear. The American Jewish Committee convened a meeting to discuss the report, and there was talk of efforts to halt the trend (Petscheck, 1985:2).

The American Jewish Committee found that it could no more "halt the trend" than it could dam a hole in the dyke with a fist. The numbers continued to climb as physical and social barriers between peoples diminished and the traditional approaches to mate selection were cast aside. Between 1920 and 1960, the Jewish intermarriage rate based on individuals was below 10 percent. By 1972, it was 30 percent and by 1980, it was 40 percent and may still be climbing (Crohn, 1986:1).

POPULATION INCREASE AND DIVERSITY

The Chinese population in New York City is predominantly foreign born. There is a vital, bustling Chinatown as a center of cultural and institutional activities. When Chinatown proper, in lower Manhattan, burst its boundaries, the overflow spilled into satellite Chinatowns in the boroughs of Queens and Brooklyn. The Chinese have established a number of strong economic bases in the restaurant business, the garment industry and the tourist trade. They have founded scores of institutions to meet their social needs. They exhibit strong ethnic pride in their cultural heritage, but there is diversity in their ranks.

Chinese immigrants no longer come from just the Canton Delta area in China. They originate from other regions of China, and the Mandarin dialect is heard in Chinatown almost as much as the Cantonese. Taiwan has a separate immigration quota of 20,000 per year, so Chinese from that island are doubling the immigrant ranks. Furthermore, the influx of Chinese refugees from Vietnam since 1975 and immigrants from Cuba, Jamaica and other

Carribean islands have swelled the numbers even more and added to the diversity.

The type of immigrants coming to the United States are different from those who came before enactment of the 1965 Immigration Act. The law gives priority to those who have close family members in the United States and to those who have skills, education and capital. As a result, the United States has creamed off large numbers of professionals, the better-educated and the monied from Taiwan, Hong Kong and Southeast Asia. However, the majority of newcomers are family members of former immigrants now joining their families. Then there is the large student group attending the city's colleges and universities. Though the socioeconomic classes are disparate, they are one in their identity as Chinese.

The ratio of Chinese men to women used to be high, but the sex ratio has evened out so that it is now balanced, especially in the marriageable age group. The factors conducive to a high in-group marriage rate such as balanced sex ratio, strong ethnic community and a large first generation population are present, but these factors are counterbalanced by the cosmopolitan environment of a city like New York.

CALCULATING THE RATES

Determining what percentage of the Chinese are marrying out depends upon how you keep score. To use a simple example, suppose two Chinese men and two Chinese women decided to marry. One couple married each other. The other two chose non-Chinese mates. In actuality, 50 percent of the group married out. Yet the coupling resulted in three marriages, one of which was an inmarriage while the other two were outmarriages. The rate based upon marriages would be 33 percent in and 67 percent out. Therefore, the intermarriage rate based upon number of marriages is always higher than that based upon number of individuals.

The intermarriage rate also tends to vary significantly between males and females. When these rates are calculated, they may differ substantially from the rates based upon total population or number of marriages. Researchers tend to talk about intermarriage rates without specifying the method of calculation. It is of the utmost importance to know the basis upon which the rates are calculated, especially when comparisons are made.

The statistics from this study come primarily from examination of the marriage license applications in the five boroughs that make up New York City. As stated previously, marriage license applications for two years, 1972 and 1982, were examined. These two years were chosen because 1982 was the latest year for which data were available when this research began. It was then arbitrarily decided to look back ten years to see if there were any discernible trends over a decade of time.

EXTENT OF INTERMARRIAGE

Tables 1A and 1B show how rates of intermarriage may be calculated. One rate is based upon number of marriages, one is calculated by dividing outmarriages by all Chinese marrying during the year, and the third breaks down the rates by sex. For example, outmarrying Chinese females are taken as a percentage of all Chinese brides for the year.

With the increase in Chinese population, the total number of outmarriages has increased between 1972 and 1982, but surprisingly, the rates have remained constant at 27 percent if number of marriages is used as a base. Calculated on the basis of percentage of individuals marrying out, the rates hover around 15 to 16 percent for both years. To see whether Chinese females or males outmarry more, the data shows that males intermarried more at 17 percent versus 15 percent for females in 1972. However, the reverse occurred in the year 1982 with females outmarrying at 16 percent versus 15 percent for the males. The differences are too slight to be significant. In essence, little change occurred over the ten year period.

TABLE 1A

CALCULATING RATES OF INTERMARRIAGE FOR CHINESE IN NEW YORK CITY

	1972		
	Inmarriage	Outmarriage	Total
Total Marriages Involving Chinese	73% (701)	27% (264)	100% 965
Total Chinese Marrying	84% (1,402)	16% (264)	100% (1,666)
Chinese Grooms	83% (701)	17% (144)	100% (845)
Chinese Brides	85% (701)	15% (120)	100% (821)

Source: New York City Marriage License Applications.

TABLE 1B

CALCULATING RATES OF INTERMARRIAGE FOR CHINESE IN NEW YORK CITY

	1982		
	Inmarriage	Outmarriage	Total
Total Marriages	73%	27%	100%
Involving Chinese	(1,067)	(390)	(1,457)
Total Chinese Marrying	85%	15%	100%
	(2,134)	(390)	(2,524)
Chinese Grooms	85%	15%	100%
	(1,067)	(181)	(1,248)
Chinese Brides	84%	16%	100%
	(1,067)	(209)	(1,276)

Source: New York City Marriage License Applications.

COMPARISON WITH HISPANIC RATES

In the subjective view of the extreme ethnocentric, even one intermarriage is one too many, but when compared to the rates of other ethnic groups, Chinese intermarriage is rather low. An excellent study by Fitzpatrick and Gurak (1979) on Hispanics in New York City provides the data for comparison. This study, also based upon marriage license applications, examined rates of outmarriage for five Hispanic groups: Puerto Ricans, South Americans, Dominicans, Central Americans and Cubans. Their findings are reproduced in Table 2 and the Chinese figures for 1972 (which is the closest year to the Hispanic study) are listed in the first column for comparison.

In this table, all three types of rates are given by marriage, by population and by sex. The most accurate is that by population, so that rate will be used for purposes of analysis and comparison. The Chinese rate is the lowest for all of the groups listed. It is 15.8 compared to 63.4 for Cubans and 29.5 for Puerto Ricans. What can explain the tremendous disparity when in many respects, the groups are similar? All of these groups are recent immigrants. They have distinctive cultural heritages and speak a foreign language. There is strong ethnic identity and cohesion within these groups, yet almost two out of three Cubans do not marry another Cuban and half of the South and Central Americans do not marry their own kind.

In a way, the high outmarriage rates for Hispanics is somewhat misleading. When they outmarry, the tendency is to marry another Hispanic albeit of

TABLE 2

INTERMARRIAGE RATES FOR CHINESE AND HISPANIC GROUPS
IN NEW YORK CITY

	Chinese	Puerto Ricans	South Americans	Dominicans	Central Americans	Cubans
Marriages	27.4	45.8	65.2	55.0	72.0	77.6
Individuals	15.8	29.5	48.4	37.9	56.1	63.4
Grooms	17.0	27.3	49.5	38.0	54.3	62.5
Brides	14.6	31.5	47.2	37.7	57.7	64.1

Note: Percentages for Chinese are for 1972; for the Hispanic groups, 1975.

Source: New York City marriage license applications. Hispanic data from Fitzpatrick and Gurak, *Hispanic Intermarriage in New York City: 1975*. New York: Fordham University Hispanic Research Center, 1979. P. 33.

another nationality. Hispanics share a common religion, a common language and a common culture. The percentage marrying into the dominant white majority is small. For Puerto Ricans, the individual rate is 12 percent; for South Americans, 16.1 percent; for Dominicans, 6 percent, for Central Americans, 23.7 percent; and for Cubans, 22.8 percent (Fitzpatrick and Gurak, 1979:35). However, when the Chinese in New York City marry out, by and large, the spouse is white rather than another Asian. Ethnicity of marital partners will be discussed later.

COMPARISON WITH CHINESE AND OTHER ASIANS IN THE WEST

Isolated studies on intermarriage have been conducted on the Chinese in California and Los Angeles, but most are now outdated. Barnett (1963) provided intermarriage rates for the Chinese in California from 1955 to 1959. He found rates, based upon marriages, ranging from 14 percent to 17 percent. Burma (1963) studied intermarriages in Los Angeles County over an eleven year period from 1948 to 1959 and found Chinese males married out at the rate of 5.8 percent and Chinese females at the rate of 4.9 percent. Again, these low rates are for the 1950s. Note that each scholar used different rates to gauge intermarriage.

The latest studies on Asian American intermarriage have been undertaken by Professor Harry Kitano and his graduate students. Their research is on Asian Americans in Los Angeles County and their data source is also marriage license applications. Their rates, based upon marriages, are given in Table 3.

TABLE 3

OUTMARRIAGE RATES OF CHINESE, JAPANESE AND KOREANS
IN LOS ANGELES, 1975, 1977 AND 1979

	1975	1977	1979
Chinese	44.0%	49.7%	41.2%
Japanese	54.8	63.1	60.6
Korean	26.0	34.1	27.6

Source: H. Kitano *et al.* "Asian American Interracial Marriage," *Journal of Marriage and the Family*,
P. 180, Table 1. February 1984.

Los Angeles is a large urban center with a sizable Asian population and a
healthy mixture of other ethnic groups, the largest being Mexican Americans.
California has had a much longer history with Asian Americans than has New
York City. The first Chinese went there during the Gold Rush. Their descen-
dants could be into the fifth generation, whereas the Chinese in New York
City are primarily first generation immigrants, with budding second and
third generations. According to Table 3, nearly half of the marriages involving
a Chinese in Los Angeles were mixed marriages in 1977. The rate declined to
41.2 percent two years later, probably reflecting an influx of immigrants and
a heightened ethnic pride and race consciousness which prevailed during
the 1970s.

What is conspicuous in Table 3 is the intermarriage rates for the Japanese.
They hover around the 60 percent level, more than double the rate of 27
percent for the Chinese in New York City and about 50 percent higher than
that for the Chinese in the same city. The factor operating here seems to be
nativity—in other words, the foreign born immigrant generation has a lower
intermarriage rate—but nativity does not wholly explain the difference. The
Japanese population in Los Angeles is 72 percent American born while the
Chinese population is only 30 percent American born according to the 1980
census. If the Japanese outmarry at 60 percent based on marriages, then the
Chinese should outmarry at only 25 percent, but they outmarried at 41
percent in 1979. What is clear from these figures for both Chinese and
Japanese is that geographic region and ethnicity are factors in the intermar-
riage pattern.

Hawaii is another area for which studies on Chinese intermarriage are
available. Because of the diversity of its population, this state has long kept
records by ethnicity, which makes it easier for social scientists to access data.
Andrew Lind, in his book *Hawaii's People* (1974), revealed that the outmarri-

age rate as early as the 1960s was already 54.8 for Chinese males and 56.8 for Chinese females. Harry Kitano *et al.* has done the latest study on this subject, and his findings are presented in Table 4.

TABLE 4

OUTMARRIAGE RATES IN HAWAII BY ASIAN GROUPS BY PERCENT
1970, 1975, AND 1980

	1970	1975	1980
Chinese	79%	79%	76%
Japanese	47	56	59
Koreans	88	90	83
Filipinos	62	65	65

Source: H. Kitano *et al.* "Asian American Interracial Marriage," *Journal of Marriage and the Family,* P. 183, Table 7. February 1984.

Comparing Los Angeles to Hawaii, the Chinese rate of intermarriage (based upon marriages) was 41.2 percent in Los Angeles in 1979 and 76 percent in Hawaii in 1980. Again, this much higher rate of outmarriage in Hawaii reflects the diverse mixture of peoples on the islands and the more accepting social climate there. The history of the Chinese people goes back to the mid-nineteenth century in Hawaii, and present-day Chinese inhabitants of the islands are well acculturated into American lifestyle and values. In Hawaii, the Chinese outmarriage rate is much higher than the Japanese one, due no doubt to their earlier history on the islands and their smaller numbers. The percentage of foreign born Chinese is only 22 percent. Immigration statistics show that few immigrants go to Hawaii. Their preference is for New York City or California, so that Chinese Americans in Hawaii are primarily American born. Generation in this country will be shown later to have a strong correlation to intermarriage.

COMPARISON WITH CENSUS STATISTICS

The United States census does provide skeletal information on intermarriage for the Chinese in its subject reports on "Marital Status" or "Marital Characteristics," usually issued in mid-decade. Statistics provided are for the nation and by regions. No breakdown is available for cities or states except for Hawaii. Figures 1 and 2 show percentages of intermarriage for husbands and wives. These figures reflect outmarriage in the whole population and include those contracted abroad or in other states as well as those contracted over

FIGURE 1

CHINESE AMERICAN INTERMARRIAGE RATES
U.S., REGIONS, AND HAWAII, 1970 AND 1980
— HUSBANDS —

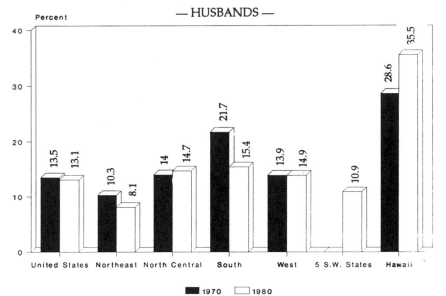

Percent

■ 1970 □ 1980

FIGURE 2

CHINESE AMERICAN INTERMARRIAGE RATES
U.S., REGIONS, AND HAWAII, 1970 AND 1980
— WIVES —

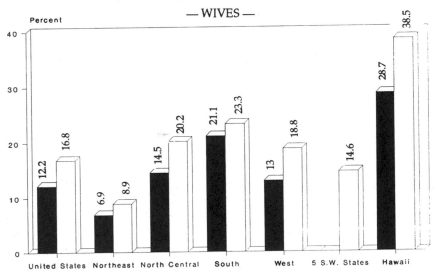

Percent

■ 1970 □ 1980

FIGURE 3

COMPARATIVE RATES OF CHINESE INTERMARRIAGE, NORTHEAST AND WESTERN REGIONS AND HAWAII, 1980

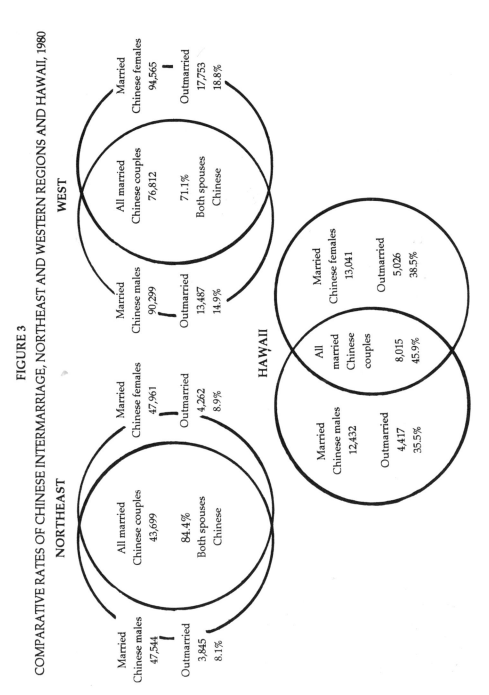

Source: U.S. Census Subject Report *Marital Characteristics*, Table 11.

the years. Census data are photos reflecting the population at a moment in time, whereas licenses show the trend taking place over time.

What these graphs disclose is that the rate of intermarriage varies greatly by region. The Northeast rates, which include New York City, are much lower than those for the other regions and are even below that for the nation. The rate at which husbands take non-Chinese spouses registers little change for 1970 and 1980, and in two regions has even declined. The picture involving wives is quite different. In every instance, there is an increase in Chinese women marrying out over the decade, although the female rates in the Northeast are exceptionally low. The overlapping circles in Figure 3 illustrate the differences in intermarriage patterns for three regions.

For this study, census data on the intermarried for New York City was extracted from the 1990 Public Use Sample tapes. Outmarriage rates for persons of Chinese ancestry based on marriages were 10 percent, based on population 5 percent, and by sex 4 percent for females and 6 percent for males. Comparable statistics for Chinese in other cities are not available, but in all likelihood, based upon data from Figures 1 and 2, other cities will have higher intermarriage rates. This confirms the contention that New York City is unlike the rest of the country in its intermarriage pattern.

Comparatives rates of intermarriage by ethnicity for the nation as a whole are available from census data, and these rates are presented in Table 5.

It is enlightening to compare the Japanese rates of intermarriage with those for the Chinese. Based on marriages, the Japanese rate is 47.7, the Chinese rate is 26.1. Based on population, the Japanese rate is 31.3; the Chinese rate is only 15. The biggest difference is for Japanese females at 40.6 percent and only 16.8 percent for Chinese. The percentage difference between Japanese and Chinese males is less—only 18.6 versus 13.1.

The Japanese are closest to the Chinese in terms of Asian background, culture and ethnic identity. Yet the intermarriage pattern is quite different. The ethnic cohesion of the Jews in New York City is somewhat similar to that of the Chinese, yet the Jews are approaching a 40 percent outmarriage rate. The recent immigration factor for both Hispanics and Chinese are similar, but it was shown in Table 2 that the Hispanic intermarriage rates in New York far exceeded that of the Chinese. Table 5 reaffirms this for the country as a whole. The next two chapters explore the characteristics of those who intermarry and the possible causal factors that could impact upon this low rate.

Sometimes it is difficult to accept the low rates for New York City at face value when intermarriages within one's own family and circle of acquaintances seem to be happening frequently. Rates are based upon a common denominator—size of population—but when that common denominator increases substantially, the actual number of intermarriages rises, even though the rates hold steady or fall.

TABLE 5

COMPARATIVE RATES OF INTERMARRIAGE IN THE UNITED STATES BY
ETHNICITY AND PERCENT, 1980

	Males	Females	Based on Total Population	Based on No. Marriages
Whites	1.1%	1.0%	1.0%	2.0%
Blacks	3.6	1.2	2.4	4.7
Japanese	18.6	40.6	31.3	47.7
Chinese	13.1	16.8	15.0	26.1
Filipinos	22.1	32.5	27.6	43.3
Spanish Origin[a]				
Mexican	16.6	16.5	16.6	28.4
Puerto Rican	26.8	24.7	25.8	41.0
Cuban	19.7	19.2	19.4	32.5
Other Sp.O.	37.5	41.4	39.5	56.7

Note: [a] Included in White and Black categories as well.

Source: U.S. Census, Subject Report, *Marital Characteristics*, 1980, Table 11.

On the other hand, the low rate is confirmed when the long-time minister of one of the largest and oldest churches in New York City's Chinatown was asked how many intermarriage ceremonies he had performed over the years. His eyebrows furrowed and he wracked his memory, but could not recall a single instance in the past. "However," he said, "I will be performing such a ceremony next week. It will be the first."

IS A TREND DISCERNIBLE?

What is the trend—up or down? Based upon the figures from a number of sources, indicators are that the rate of intermarriage for the Chinese in New York City is fairly low and is unlike that for other ethnic groups or unlike that for Chinese in other parts of the country. From 1972 to 1982, marriage license application data showed that the rates held steady at around 15 percent based on population and around 27 percent based on marriages. Elsewhere, in Los Angeles and Hawaii, the considerably higher rates have fallen off slightly. Nationally, census data show that intermarriage among the

Chinese stayed around the 15 percent level based on population and 26 percent based on marriages. The census showed an even lower rate for New York City at 10 percent based on marriages.

One of the most important variables that act upon outmarriage rates is size of the group—the smaller the group, the higher the rate. New York's Chinese population increased rapidly over the past twenty years, so with more ethnic partners available the rate of outmarriage should decline but the actual numbers will increase.

Generation is another major factor impacting on exogamy or outmarriage. The immigrant generation will hold fast to the motherland heritage and culture and will resist intermarriage strongly. The second or American born generation is more acculturated to American ways, yet will be somewhat restrained by their parents. Subsequent generations are more likely to choose their mates on the basis of personal attraction and attributes and less on the basis of nationality or ethnicity. Previous studies on intermarriage have shown that exogamy increases in direct relation to generation in the United States. Since the Chinese birthrate in New York City is low while the immigration rate is high, the first generation will predominate for some time, so the outmarriage rate should decline.

Geography seems to show a correlation with intermarriage, negatively in New York City, moderately in Los Angeles and positively in Hawaii. Events affecting Chinese Americans seem to move eastward, occurring first in the Pacific Islands, then on the West Coast, and finally on the East Coast. If the rate of intermarriage in Hawaii will eventually be replicated in New York City, then the trend will be upward.

Other factors such as the polyglot and international nature of the city, the improved economic and social status of the Chinese, the high educational attainment and the demographic dispersion away from ghettos by the middle or upper middle class Chinese, will work toward an increase in intermarriage.

Presently the rates are low and much lower than popularly perceived. Opposing forces operate at cross purposes impacting strongly on the direction of intermarriage. The stronger forces seem to be operating against exogamy in the short run and for exogamy in the long run.

3

People Who Intermarry

Even the City Clerk had to bite his lip to keep from laughing while performing the wedding ceremony for a young Chinese woman and her intended at City Hall (Case No. 1). They wanted none of the pomp and circumstances accompanying their nuptials. She wore jeans and he wore a sweatshirt. The City Clerk insisted that the bride put on a skirt. Noting that her girlfriend, who was standing up for her, was wearing a skirt, they exchanged jeans for skirt on the spot. The City Clerk then turned to the groom. Since he was not wearing a tie, they had to go to a nearby store to buy one, which the groom knotted over his sweatshirt. The City Clerk then asked for wedding rings. Both had just finished sipping Cokes. They twisted off the ring tops from the cans and handed them to the City Clerk. It was all the City Clerk could do to keep his decorum while he pronounced them man and wife.

The bride in this case was a college graduate who had lived and studied on three continents. The groom was a pre-medical student. He wore a bushy beard and a ponytail, which he had to cut when he was admitted to medical school, but not without vigorous protest. He was a White Anglo-Saxon Protestant, six feet tall and a "hippy." She was Chinese, five feet tall, and on the "hippy" side herself. Both were community activists during the 1970s. They have been married for eleven years, but have separated on several occasions. They have one child.

Steve is a tall, lanky Chinese man married to Fumiko, a short, plump Japanese woman (Case No. 42). Poetry is the cement that attracted them to each other and still binds them. He was born in Hong Kong, she in an internment camp during World War II. They are both college educated, literary people, but Steve works as a shirt dyer in a factory. After hours, he works on his novel. Fumiko is older than Steve. They have a "healthy, loving, caring relationship." They have one child and have been married thirteen years. When asked to rate their marriage on a scale of one to ten, with ten being the most positive, they agreed that it was a 9.5.

It is hard to see why Henry and Chu-ling are married, yet they have been together for thirteen years (Case No. 45). Chu-ling says, "I hate white men."

When asked why she married Henry, she admits, "I love him." Henry is Jewish. Chu-ling has mixed Chinese blood. The cement that binds, in this case, despite all the contradictions in terms of personality, background and temperament, is their common fight against Third-World oppression. They both work ceaselessly for the cause, making it their lifework and careers. Both had been married previously, Henry to another Jewish woman, Chu-ling to a black physicist. Her first marriage was for expediency's sake. "I needed the green card for permanent residence," she admitted. Both are highly creative personalities. Chu-ling has attended some of the most prestigious schools in the United States, but she is the product of the rebellious seventies. In China, where she grew up, she had all the advantages of a privileged upbringing, but in her usual forthright manner she said, "I hate my mother." Both Henry and Chu-ling are rebels to the core. A year after the interview, Chu-ling and Henry separated.

Who are the people who intermarry? What are they like in terms of temperament, class, sex, age, ethnicity of spouse, marital history and so forth?

Theorists are of two schools regarding people who intermarry. Either they are rebels, neurotics, self-haters, social climbers, or they are vanguards, trend setters, innovators, adventurers, the courageous. Without doubt, they are an unconventional lot who are not bothered by public opinion. Rebellion seems to be a fairly common characteristic of the intermarried. They may be rebelling against family, society, racism, institutional conventions or the past. Even when they are not angry against anyone or the world, they are forced, in most cases, to go against the wishes of their families. There are no data to substantiate the instances where couples backed out of intermarriage in the face of family opposition, but in the case histories from interviews for this study, the lengths of courtships suggest protracted struggles against parental opposition. In some instances, the couples waited eight, ten, even twenty-five years to get married. These were strong-willed people.

The least likely rebel (Case No. 47) was extremely soft-spoken, tall, willowy and feminine. She said she met her husband at a time when the civil rights confrontations were at their height in the South. She felt indignation when she saw young students barred from colleges in Little Rock, Arkansas because of the color of their skin. "I became acutely aware of the injustices of prejudice and discrimination," she said. "I wanted to transcend the color bar."

Self-haters? That is much too strong a word. People who are attracted to members of the opposite sex of another race do not hate themselves. It is just that they have been socialized to view certain physical, social and personality traits as more attractive and more desirable than those found in members of their own ethnic group. For example, by American standards, female beauty includes blonde hair, blue eyes, fair skin, bosomy chest, long legs, thin nostrils, and round, deep-set eyes. Attractive males, are tall, strong, muscular

and have angular features. They are brave, aggressive, protective, consider-
ate. The impression of what is attractive comes from television exposure,
movie magazines, commercial advertisements, books and films. Yet the usual
physique of the Chinese male is short, thin and slight. He is quiet and
reticent, while the Chinese female has black hair, olive-skin, flatter chest,
shorter legs and rounder nostrils.

Constant reinforcement through the media of what is beautiful and what
are desired standards of behavioral traits has internalized these concepts
within the minds of Chinese Americans who were brought up in this country
or who have extensive exposure to Western ideals. If this concept is difficult
to accept, just think: how was it that for centuries Chinese men became
erotically aroused at the sight of "four-inch lilies," which were, in essence,
grotesquely bound female feet? In certain African tribes, women elongate
their necks by wearing neck rings that stretch their heads above their
shoulders. Others wear lip rings to force the protrusion of lower lips. Small
feet, long necks, thick lips were the beauty features in these cultures.

Excerpts from the poem, "I Hate My Wife for Her Flat Yellow Face,"
(Tanaka, 1969) reveals the dichotomy of this Asian man's feelings:

> I hate my wife for her flat yellow face
> and her fat cucumber legs, but mostly
> for her lack of elegance and lack of
> intelligence compared to judith gluck . . . .
>
> She's like a stupid water buffalo from
> the old country, slowly plodding between
> muddy furrows, and that's all she knows of
> love beneath my curses and sometimes blows . . . .
>
> I thought I could love her at first, that she
> could teach me to be myself again, free
> from years of bopping around LA ghettos,
> western civilization and the playmate of the month . . . .
>
> But I wanted to be anglican
> too much and listened too long to dylan
> or maybe it was the playmate of the
> month or poetry and judith gluck . . . .

In kind, "Oriental girls do not want to be plagued with the short, ugly,
unconfident, clumsy, arrogant, Oriental man." (Anonymous, 1969). On the

other hand, other stereotypes laudatory about the Chinese are in the minds of the non-Chinese partners. Chinese women are petite, soft, feminine, gentle, obedient, loving and submissive. The males are good family men, reliable, steady, smart and do not get drunk.

HIGHER SOCIOECONOMIC STATUS

Is intermarriage occurring among the upper socioeconomic classes? Some evidence points in that direction. First, using 1980 census data to buttress the argument, it was found that 55 percent of the Chinese men who outmarried had some college education as compared to only 29 percent of those who inmarried. The more spectacular statistic is that 67 percent of non-Chinese men who married Chinese wives had some college background. As for the women, of Chinese wives who married out, 72 percent had some college education compared to only 20 percent who married in. The percentage of non-Chinese wives who married Chinese men is 35 (*See,* Table 6). In other words, Chinese women who marry out are better educated than non-Chinese women marrying Chinese men.

TABLE 6

COLLEGE EDUCATION OF CHINESE IN NEW YORK CITY, BY PERCENT, 1980

		College			
	N = 100%	1–3 Years	4 Years	Post Graduate	Total
Inmarriage					
Chinese Husbands	1,233	8%	10%	11%	29%
Outmarriage	137				
Chinese Husbands	80	30	14	11	55
Non-Chinese Husbands	57	18	21	28	67
Inmarriage					
Chinese Wives	1,233	7	7	6	20
Outmarriage	137				
Chinese Wives	57	23	23	26	72
Non-Chinese Wives	80	16	9	10	35

Source: U.S. Census Public Use Sample Data.

The second leg of a socioeconomic index is income. In Table 7, the three upper levels of family income recorded by the census for Chinese in New York City have been tabulated for Chinese husband/Chinese wife families, Chinese husband/non-Chinese wife families and Chinese wife/non-Chinese husband families. Family income is generally dominated by earnings of the husband, though perhaps not when the wife is well-educated. The income figures reveal startling disparities. When the family is headed by a Chinese husband, only 11 percent in both in and outmarriages exceeded $35,000 in 1979, whereas when the husband is non-Chinese, 39 percent of the families reported upper level incomes.

TABLE 7

CHINESE FAMILIES WITH UPPER LEVEL FAMILY INCOME, IN NEW YORK CITY, BY PERCENT, 1979

	Chinese Husband Chinese Wife	Chinese Husband Non-Chinese Wife	Chinese Wife Non-Chinese Husband
$35,000–39,999	3%	1%	9%
$40,000–49,999	4	5	19
$50,000 plus	4	5	11
Total	11%	11%	39%
100%	(1,233)	(80)	(57)

Source: U.S. Census Public Use Sample Data.

In interpreting the figures for families headed by non-Chinese husbands, however, one must consider the high educational level and occupational status of the Chinese wives. In all likelihood, these families would be two income ones, thus bolstering total family income.

Using occupation as the third indicator, it seems that those who intermarry have higher status careers. Using 1980 census data on married couples involving Chinese in New York City and taking the two top occupational categories—Executives or Administrators and Professional or Technical—one sees that the percentage differences are quite pronounced for those who inmarried versus those who outmarried (See, Table 8). The difference is 10 percentage points or 23 percent for Chinese men who married in versus 33 percent for those who married out. Non-Chinese husbands with Chinese wives exceed both the other groups with 46 percent in the upper occupational classifications.

The differences in percentages for the wives is even more spectacular. Only 9 percent of inmarried Chinese wives are in the two top occupational categories compared to 36 percent of outmarried Chinese wives. In this instance,

TABLE 8

CHINESE IN TOP OCCUPATIONAL CATEGORIES, IN NEW YORK CITY,
BY PERCENT, 1980

	N = 100%	Executive Administrative	Professional Technical	Total
Inmarriage				
Chinese Husbands	1,233	12%	11%	23%
Outmarriage	137			
Chinese Husbands	80	13	20	33
Non-Chinese Husbands	57	16	30	46
Inmarriage				
Chinese Wives	1,233	4	5	9
Outmarriage	137			
Chinese Wives	57	11	25	36
Non-Chinese Wives	80	4	14	18

Source: U.S. Census Public Use Sample Data.

18 percent of non-Chinese wives of Chinese men are in these upper occupational groups, but they are outpaced by outmarried Chinese wives.

While the figures for 1982, obtained from marriage license information shown in Table 9, indicate changes in some areas, it confirms the trend depicted above.

The figures for education, occupation and income point to higher socio-economic levels for intermarried couples. Various social scientists have also commented on the higher socioeconomic level of the intermarried in other groups. In their research summary on Hispanics, Fitzpatrick and Gurak (1979) remarked, "We have fairly consistent evidence that exogamy is associated with higher occupational status, that this is more true for brides than for grooms, and that exogamous brides, who already possess higher status occupations than do endogamous brides, are more likely to marry spouses with relatively higher statuses than are their endogamous counterparts." Egon Mayer (1985), in reference to Jews who intermarry, found that they tend to be better educated and higher achievers. Paul Glick (1970), well-known demographer from the U.S. Census Bureau, wrote: "The selective process in Negro-white intermarriage often involved Negroes with more education than those who had married another Negro and white persons with less education than those who had married another white person" (p. 294).

TABLE 9
TOP LEVEL OCCUPATIONS OF CHINESE APPLYING
FOR MARRIAGE LICENSES, BY PERCENT, 1982

	N = 100%	Executive Administrative	Professional Technical	Total
Inmarriage				
Chinese Husbands	1,029	6%	22%	28%
Outmarriage	321			
Chinese Husbands	149	7	30	37
Non-Chinese Husbands	172	10	36	46
Inmarriage				
Chinese Wives	1,036	4	16	20
Outmarriage	279			
Chinese Wives	129	16	24	40
Non-Chinese Wives	150	5	22	27

Source: New York City Marriage License Bureau.

The only scholars with findings contrary to the above were Kitano and Yeung (1982), referring to the Chinese in Los Angeles in 1979. Their data reveal that "inmarried males show a higher proportion in the college graduate and graduate school level than the outmarried males." The mean educational level for the inmarried Chinese groom was 16.1, for the outmarried groom, 15.4. For inmarried Chinese brides, the mean educational level was 15.1; for the outmarried, it was 14.7. Neither of these differences were statistically significant. One factor that could have skewed these results is the unusually high educational attainment of the Chinese in the United States, in particular the large numbers of foreign students who come here for graduate studies. For example, 39 percent of all Chinese males age 25–54 have 16+ years of schooling. This percentage for Chinese females is 37 percent (East-West, 1986). In time, the Chinese pattern should reveal a positive correlation of higher socioeconomic status with intermarriage.

AGE FACTOR

Are Chinese who intermarry from the younger age brackets or the older? One conjecture is that they will be older because of delay in marital plans for reasons of education or career. As noted above, the outmarried do tend to be better educated, have higher status occupations and earn more money. Another theory advanced is that these people sought someone within their own ethnic group originally but did not succeed in finding a mate. As time went by and the eligibles within the smaller ethnic group thinned out, they had to look elsewhere for marital partners. The opposite supposition is that younger people are more receptive to social change and unconventional ways, thus more likely to marry out at a higher rate.

Social scientists are divided on the age issue. D.Y. Yuan (1980:187), using 1970 census data, asserted that "there is a strong inverse relationship between age and the proportion intermarried . . . ." In other words, the younger Chinese marry out more. Yuan shows that the 20 to 24 year age group has the highest intermarriage rate, and with each increase in age group, there is a decrease in outmarriage.

Kitano and Yeung (1982), using Los Angeles County marriage license data, found that the percentage of outmarried Chinese males in the under 25 age group was 35.7 percent compared to 20 percent for the inmarried group. In the same age group for females, the percentage was about 46 percent for both the in and outmarried. These findings suggest that the young are more likely to marry out.

In this study of the Chinese in New York City, the age at time of marriage for brides and grooms in both in and outmarriages for the year 1982 have been plotted in Figures 4 and 5. The data suggest that those who marry out are slightly older than those who marry in. The most prevalent age of marriage for both brides and grooms is in the 25 to 29 year old category. Figure 4 for grooms shows that the in and outmarried lines closely follow one another except that exogamous grooms marry slightly later, and then there is another jump within the 40 to 45 year old age category.

Figure 5 for brides shows that Chinese females definitely marry later when they marry out. The broken line is invariably higher than the solid line. Figures 6 and 7 plot the intermarriage pattern by age for 1972 and 1982. These figures reveal that there have been significant changes over the ten year period. Without doubt, brides and grooms marrying out more recently are tying the knot at a more mature stage in life. The most dramatic change is for outmarrying Chinese brides, where the divergence of lines is quite pronounced, confirming that when Chinese marry out, they do so when they are older. These findings corroborate studies done on Korean Americans, Jews and Hispanics.

Kitano and Chai (1982) state, in their study of Korean intermarriage: "In general, for Korean Americans, the males who outmarry tend to be older than the Korean males who chose Korean brides." For example, only 10 percent of Korean men in the 41 to 50 age bracket married in comparison to 21 percent

FIGURES 4 AND 5

AGE AT TIME OF IN AND OUTMARRIAGE, CHINESE BRIDES AND GROOMS,
NEW YORK CITY, BY PERCENT, 1982

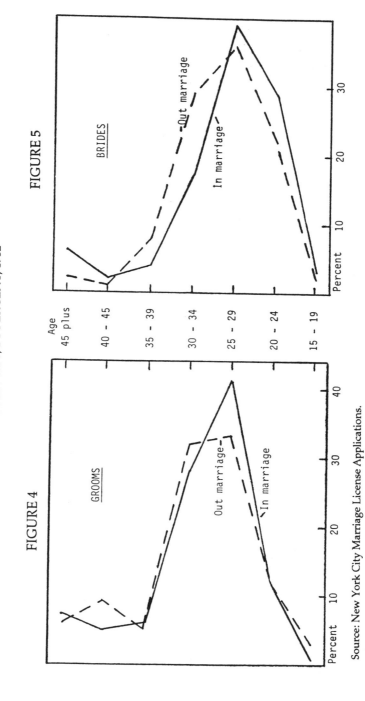

FIGURE 5

FIGURE 4

Source: New York City Marriage License Applications.

FIGURE 6

AGE AT TIME OF OUTMARRIAGE, CHINESE GROOMS, NEW YORK CITY, BY PERCENT 1972 AND 1982

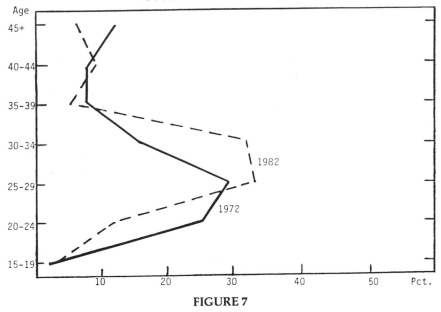

FIGURE 7

AGE AT TIME OF OUTMARRIAGE, CHINESE BRIDES, NEW YORK CITY, BY PERCENT 1972 AND 1982

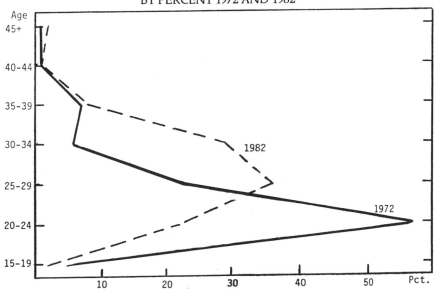

Source: New York City Marriage License Applications.

of Korean men who married out. The picture was the same for Korean women. In the same age bracket, 3.3 percent married in; 8.2 percent married out.

In a study of Jewish intermarriage, Egon Mayer (1985) found that "Disproportionately, intermarriers are also people who marry at a somewhat later age than those who marry within their own ethnic and religious groups." Louis Berman (1968) in *Jews and Intermarriage*, finds the same as Egon Mayer.

According to a study of Hispanics in New York City by Fitzpatrick and Gurak (1979), "Both age at marriage and remarriage status are predictably, positively associated with intermarriage . . . While Hispanics marry for the first time at older ages than do average Americans, this appears to be a function of disruptions of life cycle timing caused by the migration process. Among second generation Hispanics, only the South and Central Americans continue to marry at ages older than the national average." However, Mittelbach *et al.* (1966), in their study of Mexican Americans in Los Angeles, found that it is the younger males who marry out.

The correlation of age with intermarriage seems to vary with ethnic group, time and place. With the Chinese in New York, the trend seems to lean toward greater maturity, especially with Chinese females. Figures 6 and 7 definitely establish that fact.

GENERATION

If there is one finding that scholars who have studied the intermarriage phenomenon agree upon, it is that generation has a direct correlation with the rate at which ethnic groups marry out. In other words, the American born or second generation is more likely to marry out than the immigrant first generation, and subsequent native born generations like the third or fourth are even more likely to do so. Table 10 presents data for in and outmarriage rates for the Chinese marrying in New York City for the years 1972 and 1982 by birthplace. Note that Chinese born in China, Taiwan or Hong Kong have very low intermarriage rates. Approximately nine out of ten marry within their national group. These people undoubtedly have a strong sense of their Chinese identity and would be reluctant to compromise it.

However, first generation Chinese born in other countries such as Malaysia, Indonesia, the Philippines and Latin American countries exhibit less reluctance to take mates from other national groups. Perhaps this reflects the more tolerant stance toward intermarriage from the land of their former residence. The contrast is quite sharp. For example, 9 percent of Chinese grooms born in China, Taiwan or Hong Kong married out in 1982, whereas 32 percent of those born in other countries did so. For Chinese brides, the

TABLE 10

IMPACT OF GENERATION UPON IN OR OUTMARRIAGE FOR CHINESE IN NEW YORK CITY, BY PERCENT, 1972 AND 1982

Generation	1972		
	Inmarriage	Outmarriage	N = 100%
Chinese Groom			
1—Born China/TW/HK[a]	86%	14%	678
1—Born Other Country	63	37	27
2—Born United States	80	20	82
Chinese Bride			
1—Born China/TW/HK	94	6	586
1—Born Other Country	81	19	37
2—Born United States	69	31	129

	1982		
Chinese Groom			
1—Born China/TW/HK[a]	91%	9%	1,010
1—Born Other Country	68	32	62
2—Born United States	69	31	112
Chinese Bride			
1—Born China/TW/HK	92	8	995
1—Born Other Country	76	24	75
2—Born United States	66	34	97

Note: [a] Taiwan and Hong Kong

Source: New York City Marriage License Applications.

percentages are 8 versus 24. Obviously, the generation label has to be modified. It is no longer just immigrant versus American born generations; consideration must also be given to country of origin.

Confirmation is provided by the data that American born Chinese Americans definitely marry out at a higher rate than those from China, Taiwan and Hong Kong. One out of three did so in 1982, and the trend is up from 1972, especially with the grooms. Explanation for this lies in the fact that the American born generations are more acculturated to American ways and

American values, and this factor will impact even more heavily upon subsequent generations. However, the Chinese population in New York City is still very much a first generation one. Three out of four were born abroad, and the birth rate is very low. Consequently, the rate of intermarriage in New York City will remain low until a substantial second or third generation cohort evolves.

ETHNICITY OF MARRIAGE PARTNER

Although the United States has well-defined national boundaries, an ethnic American is an elusive concept. Ethnic identity in terms of the country of ancestral origin remains strong or the division may be along lines of race or religion. Thus, a person is identified as black, Jewish, Italian American or Chinese American in spite of the fact that his or her roots may go deep into American soil. If an American black marries an American Jew, that is an intermarriage, despite the fact that both spouses may be fifth generation Americans. White Catholics marrying white Protestants are defined in the same way. For Chinese Americans, the lines are especially clear cut. They are a national ethnic group with distinctive cultural traits, and they are a racial minority with identifiable physical features. Thus, any person of Chinese blood or heritage who takes a spouse of a different nationality or race has entered into an intermarriage.

In this study, ethnic identification, taken from marriage license applications, based primarily on surname or birthplace, was simple for some groups and difficult or impossible for others. There was no way to tell blacks from whites. Names such as McDougal, Brown and Jones could have been either. That is why no attempt was made to delineate color or religion except for Jews. Although researchers were armed with a list of common Jewish names, it was still hard to be sure. Jackson? There are blacks, whites and Jews by that name. Perhaps that is why our count of Jews as Chinese marital partners was lower than expected. Hispanic, Japanese, Vietnamese and Korean names were more easily identifiable. In this study, Chinese marrying another Asian was also classified as intermarried.

Table 11 shows ethnicity of the marital partners from the marriage license applications for 1972 and 1982.

Endogamy, or inmarriage, remains overwhelmingly the dominant pattern for the Chinese in New York City. Counting mixed Chinese who tend to be raised as Chinese, the percentage of inmarriage ranges from 85 to 88 percent. Inmarriage rates remained fairly constant over the ten year period. Any increase in Chinese male outmarriages came when they married other Asians. The increase in Chinese female outmarriages occurred when they married into the white, black and "others" categories, but, undoubtedly, most were

TABLE 11

ETHNICITY OF MARITAL PARTNERS OF THE CHINESE
IN NEW YORK CITY, 1972, 1982

	1972		1982	
	Number	Percent	Number	Percent
Chinese Groom				
married to:				
Chinese	668	83	1,038	86
Mixed Chinese	14	2	13	1
White, Black, Others	69	9	64	5
Hispanic	43	5	34	3
Jewish	0	0	3	—
Japanese	2	—	6	1
Korean	4	1	21	2
Indo-Chinese	1	—	22	2
Total	801	100	1,201	100
Chinese Bride				
married to:				
Chinese	668	86	1,038	85
Mixed Chinese	17	2	13	1
White, Black, Others	84	11	131	11
Hispanic	7	1	18	1
Jewish	0	0	11	1
Japanese	0	0	5	—
Korean	3	—	0	0
Indo-Chinese	1	—	9	1
Total	780	100	1,225	100

Source: New York City Marriage License Applications.

with white grooms. Black husbands were not uncommon. From the 50 case histories of those interviewed, three Chinese women were married to black men, another was previously married to a black man, and yet another lived with a black man for an extended period of time.

Black Spouses

Jade is a third generation Chinese American (Case No. 47). She is in her mid-50s. Her husband, Tom, was born in Brooklyn. They met at graduate school in upstate New York. According to Jade, at that time it was very unusual for a black person to be in graduate school. Jade was already engaged to a Chinese boy back home in the West. But Tom swept her off her feet. When she met Tom, Jade was also dating a Chinese professor at the university. She broke her engagement to her fiance, "an act that caused him a long bout of illness." In comparison with Tom, the Chinese professor seemed insipid. She married Tom over the strong protests of her family who disowned her. They said, "Come home. Let us talk to you one more time. If you choose to go through with it, then you have to understand that we won't have anything to do with you, and you won't be Chinese any more because you have to live with them and live a black life." Jade decided to proceed. She said, "It bothered me for a year or so, but I decided I was strong enough to do it." Jade has been married for 32 years now and is the mother of seven children.

Thelma is second generation Chinese American, born and raised in the Midwest (Case No. 36). She is also in her mid-50s. As a giddy teenager, she idolized a Chinese fellow who eventually married a white girl. She admits that all the men in her life look more or less like her first love. Subconsciously, she felt that "if he can marry a Caucasian, I can too." At twenty, she married a French man. That marriage ended in a friendly divorce. She has been married for the past 26 years to a Caribbean black. Her husband, Noel, emphasizes his Caribbean heritage over his blackness, but Thelma and their daughter have forced Noel to come to terms with his race. Noel is light-skinned and Thelma "looks like a Filipina, so sometimes people think we are a Filipino couple." However, the daughter is fiercely proud of her black blood, and Thelma is a civil rights activist and articulate spokesperson on minority issues. "Noel looks like my Chinese boyfriend," said Thelma. "As soon as I saw him, I set my trap for him." Both Thelma and Noel are college graduates.

Elizabeth was born in New York's Chinatown (Case No. 4). She has a Master's degree in education and teaches in the city's public schools. Her romance took place under the swaying palms of the Caribbean where she had gone for her vacation. George worked in the kitchen of the hotel where she was staying, but he had put on an art show for the tourists and Elizabeth was very much taken by his creativity and artistry. She said, "At the end of the week, I thought that it would end and that there would be nothing further. We wrote to each other, and he surprised me by coming to New York for a visit. We visited his aunt, and I found that they were well-educated, professional people. George is 6'2", personable, well-liked and has lots of empathy for other people. We are very much alike in this respect. My thoughts were: Chinese men are never that way. I had just broken off with a Chinese boy before going on my vacation, and I wasn't going to sit around waiting for a Chinese man. I was already over thirty. I never thought that color was such a great barrier. Would you believe I went down twelve times to see him before we tied the knot?" George and Elizabeth have been married seventeen years and they have one son.

In each of these instances, one can see that these women actively pursued the men that they married and the marriages have been successful in spite of the tremendous barriers that they had to overcome.

Hispanic Spouses

What did prove surprising was that so many Chinese married persons of Hispanic origin. In 1972, 43 Chinese men chose Hispanic women as brides; in 1982, 34 did so. Fewer Chinese women took Hispanic mates, but in comparison with marriage to spouses of other ethnic groups, Hispanics still ranked high. In recollection, the Chinese-Hispanic marriage license applications came from the Bronx, where there are large Hispanic populations. Among our interviewees, there were only three cases. One marriage was contracted in South America, one was with a Spaniard in Europe and the third took place in New York City. All three cases conformed to the highly educated profile. However, this writer also came across three cases (not interviewed because social service agencies would not reveal their identities) that involved young teenagers who met and married in high school. None of these marriages survived and they became case loads for social service agencies.

The Chinese-Hispanic attraction may be explained in part by Chinese who have been immigrating from Latin America and the Caribbean. Some may have been Chinese who first went to Latin America, who speak the Spanish language and who made a second migration to the United States. In New York, there is a concentration of Cuban Chinese along upper Broadway. They operate restaurants that sell black beans and rice, tacos and plantains. On the Lower East Side, Puerto Ricans and Chinese are the largest ethnic groups. In the schools, the young people have ample opportunity to come into contact. Besides, there are 1.5 million people of Spanish origin in the five counties of New York City. Undoubtedly the size of the Hispanic population is one factor. Others, as pointed out, are proximity and secondary migration.

Jewish Spouses

Jews are another dominant ethnic group in New York City. In fact, their numbers are more than twice that of Hispanics. Since Jewish and Chinese values are quite similar (for example, both groups are strongly family-oriented, they value education, they are hard-working and upwardly mobile), it was expected that Chinese would more likely marry Jews if they out-married. Data from the marriage license applications did not reveal this. The reason, however, may be chalked up to the difficulty of identifying Jews by surname, and since many are beyond third-generation, they cannot be pin-pointed by parents' place of birth. Even when that is possible, they may have emigrated from countries like France, Russia or Estonia, in which case they would have been categorized as white Caucasian. Among the interviewees, however, six Chinese women married Jewish men and two Chinese men married Jewish women, reaffirming the belief that there is a special marital attraction between Chinese and Jews.

Other Asian Spouses

On the East coast, Chinese are not likely to intermarry with other Asians, although such is not the case in Hawaii or the West coast. There, Chinese-Japanese unions are more common. Gurak and Kritz (1978), who studied patterns of Hispanic intermarriage, discovered that intermarriage occurs within clusters of closely related or cultural groups. For example, there is a very strong tendency for Hispanics to marry one another even though they are of different national origin. The pattern also holds for Slavics, Scandina-vians and Anglo-Saxons. A slight increase of Chinese marrying other Asians is apparent in New York City from 1972 to 1982, and the increase occurs more with Chinese men taking other Asian brides. This may be a result of the large influx of refugees from Vietnam who may have used Vietnamese spelling of their names, but who are ethnically Chinese. Among the respondents who were interviewed, two Chinese men took Japanese wives, and one Chinese woman took a Japanese husband. No Chinese married Koreans, Filipinos, or Vietnamese. One couple consisted of a mixed blood Asian Indian/European man and a Chinese woman and, even more surprising, this writer came across an instance of an American Indian man married to a Chinese woman, al-though information about the latter came indirectly through a social service agency. The couple was not interviewed.

It is quite apparent that intermarriage among the Chinese is not just a two ethnic group combination, but a multifaceted one with marital partners of many nationalities and races, in many ways reflecting the ethnic diversity that is New York City.

REMARRIAGE

A popular supposition is that people who intermarry have had previous marriages. There is some truth to this statement. Former marriages may have ended with death or divorce. The marital history of applicants for marriage licenses in New York City for 1972 and 1982 are given in Table 12. In 1972, 11 percent of the Chinese men marrying out had been previously married, whereas the percentage for those marrying in was slightly less at 9 percent. For Chinese brides, it was a different story. For 24 percent of those marrying out, it was the second time around versus 8 percent for those marrying within the group. The pattern held for the year 1982 except that the percentage for remarriage for brides marrying out was lowered to 15 percent.

Two reasons can be advanced for the higher remarriage rate for the intermarried. As has already been pointed out, these people feel less constrained by public opinion and are more receptive to change. Secondly, as it pertains especially to women, there is the stigma of remarriage. Chinese men are reluctant to marry women who have been married before. Even when widowed, Chinese women are supposed to remain true to their deceased husbands. In China, the countryside is dotted with arches built in honor of such virtuous widows. To remarry, Chinese women find it easier to go outside their own ethnic group.

From the fifty intermarried cases interviewed in this study, one non-Chinese and seven Chinese women had been married once before. Two non-Chinese and four Chinese men were previously wed. All these men were divorced. Two of the women were widowed. One hesitates to conclude whether these divorce rates are on the high side or low side considering that American divorces are now half of the numbers marrying.

The usual response to an unhappy union for the Chinese is to think of it as one's lot and to endure. However, while divorce might bring feelings of guilt, some see it as the correct choice. Flora (Case No. 20) was an extremely outgoing, intelligent woman. She was inquisitive, sensitive and eager to learn. Yet, at age 17, a matchmaker brought a picture of a handsome young man to her family in Connecticut, and the two were married. "All the marriages in my family were arranged," said Flora. "There were no other Chinese families in Connecticut, so when we became of age, my mother sent for the matchmaker. My first husband was China born. He came from a scholarly family, but he could only find work in a laundry and then in a restaurant. All my sisters thought I had the greatest marriage. He was good looking. He took the kids to the park. He helped with the housework. But we kept drifting apart. I had to stay Chinese for my husband, but I liked American things. I like to read movie magazines, the society column. I wanted to go to plays, but my husband only liked cowboy or action movies. And then I had to translate for him. I wanted to go to night school. He felt threatened by that. I wanted the divorce, but I felt guilty about it. He really was a nice guy."

Flora's second husband is Jewish, a chemical engineer and a sculptor. She was attracted by his artistic talents. At first, she supported him so he could

TABLE 12

MARITAL HISTORY OF CHINESE BRIDES AND GROOMS IN
NEW YORK CITY, 1972 AND 1982

	1972							
	Groom				Bride			
Previous Marriages	Inmarriage		Outmarriage		Inmarriage		Outmarriage	
	No.	Pct.	No.	Pct.	No.	Pct.	No.	Pct.
None	637	91	117	89	642	92	55	76
One	59	8	15	11	52	7	17	24
Two	4	1	0	0	5	1	0	0
Three	1	—	0	0	2	—	0	0
Total	701	100	132	100	701	100	72	100
	1982							
None	916	89	160	87	959	92	138	85
One	75	7	14	8	77	7	24	15
Two	40	4	9	5	8	1	2	—
Three	3	—	0	0	2	—	0	0
Total	1,034	100	183	100	1,036	100	162	100

Note: Persons of mixed Chinese blood counted as Chinese.

Source: New York City Marriage License Applications.

devote full time to his art. She went back to school for her Bachelor's and Master's degrees. Now she is going to law school.

ARTISTIC ATTRACTION

It is uncanny how many of the interviewees for this study were attracted to their mates by their artistic bent. This was a factor for six couples and probably indicates a creative tendency in people who depart from the norm. Consider the case of Julia (Case No. 44) who had gone to Taiwan to teach English. She met Liang at a New Year's party at his place. He had sent out handmade invitations. Julia was taken by the artistic invitations, but at the party she was fascinated by the way Liang seemingly spoke with his hands. That attraction still holds. The couple are in New York now. Liang worked as a commercial artist, but when the baby came, Julia urged Liang to stay home so he could take care of the baby and have more time to devote to his painting while she continues work. Both Flora and Julia want to encourage their husbands' artistic talents and are willing to support them in their pursuits.

AN ASIAN ATTRACTION

In recent years, Americans have taken on a special fascination with things Asian. Julia, mentioned above, said her identity was always tied to Asia. She studied Chinese at the University of Kansas and then at the special language school in Middlebury, Vermont. When her father died and she came into some insurance money, she and her younger sister went to Taiwan. She came back to the United States to finish her degree, but immediately went back to Taiwan to teach. Julia speaks Mandarin better than a native. Julia and Liang are now planning to go live in China.

Frank's major at Seton Hall University in New Jersey was Chinese history. He planned to go into the foreign service. Frank and Ching-li's home (Case No. 33) has shelves lined with books and magazines on China. Frank speaks fluent Mandarin. He knows more about Chinese culture, history and philosophy than do most Chinese men.

Gordon (Case No. 47) is equally conversant in Cantonese and Mandarin, having lived in Hong Kong for many years. He met Mei-Hwa in the Far East, but did not marry her until they were reunited in New York where she had come to study. Mei-Hwa said, "I know a lot about his culture and he knows a lot about mine." Gordon is an anthropologist.

CONCLUSION

People who intermarry have special characteristics and traits. In New York City, at least, they tend to be better educated, have professional or managerial jobs and have higher incomes than people who marry their own kind. Other social scientists have documented the higher socioeconomic level of intermarrieds as well. Because they must spend more time achieving their higher status, they postpone marriage until a later age. This is more apparent with Chinese females than males.

As a rule, the immigrant generation clings to its old values and traditions and is not as likely to wed outside of its own group. However, if the first generation to come to the United States has already made an intermediary move from their native homeland to another region such as Southeast Asia or Latin America and then migrates again to the United States, the rate of intermarriage is much higher. It resembles or even exceeds the rate for American born Chinese, who are acculturated and who have an American outlook and American values. Since three out of four Chinese in New York City were born abroad, the Chinese in New York City are very much a first generation people. Combined with a low birthrate, the rate of intermarriage will remain low. The numbers, however, will increase as the population increases.

As for the ethnicity of marital partners in Chinese intermarriages, they seem to be all over the map. From the interviewees alone, there were representatives from every continent except Australia and Antarctica—Brazilian, Swedish, Hungarian, Yugoslavian, Italian, German, Irish, Asian Indian, Lebanese, Scottish, Puerto Rican, Spanish, Japanese, American black and Caribbean black, although American Caucasian Protestants and Jews predominated. Under such circumstances, intermarriage is not a two culture union, but a multicultural one.

People who intermarry tend to be nonconformist or nontraditional, and they also tend to be marrying for the second or more time. They are willing to make changes and appear unconventional. Non-Chinese taking Chinese spouses may already have laid the groundwork for their actions by exhibiting an interest or fascination with things Chinese. By putting themselves in a social or physical setting conducive to meeting Chinese, they increase the odds of marrying Chinese.

4

Drawing Magnets

Variations on the theme of love are the building blocks of much of the world's literature. Love stories never lose their hold to entertain and to plumb the depths of human emotions. Tales of how boy meets girl and falls in love are endless. When the path of love does not run smooth the story is even more exciting. The wider the distance between the two, socially, culturally or otherwise, the better the story. This theme is reflected in Cinderella stories where Prince Charming marries a lowly maiden. Another popular theme is mirrored in the Romeo and Juliet stories where love meets insurmountable barriers and ends in tragedy. Both these themes are undercurrents in Chinese American intermarriages.

What magnetic force attracts and draws a man and woman together, especially since the origins of these couples may have been tens of thousands of miles apart? What draws together two individuals from different cultures and backgrounds? How does a man or woman from the other side of the globe end up in matrimony with someone on this side of the earth? The obstacles of legal obstruction, centuries old tradition, cultural differences, family objection and societal aversion are no less formidable in Chinese American mixed marriages. Yet at times Cupid does triumph.

Among our interviewees the love stories are there, although the original intent of the participants may not have been romantic nor the purpose matrimony. As Irving (Case No. 9) said, "I met her (Melody) in the elevator. I saw her a couple of times before I asked her for a date. She was pretty." From Melody's perspective, how did the relationship develop? "Casual at first. I didn't have many friends in New York. I liked having someone to go out with. He was easy to talk to. I didn't view it as a long-term relationship at that time. I never thought I would marry a non-Chinese. Irving can start a conversation easily. At that time I was not very outgoing. I admired that quality. He took an interest in me. I felt comfortable with him. It was a matter of time. He respected me. He's not chauvinistic. That makes a difference. I'm very comfortable with him."

In a matter-of-fact manner, Kenneth (Case No. 38) tells his story: "We were both foreign students, Sonia from Europe and I from China. We met at an international student meeting, and I asked her to get me a beer. Sonia is not a beauty, but she was tall, blonde and slim. At that time, there were few Chinese girls around, and they were all snobbish, especially those from Shanghai. Before you date them, they want to know whether you are a doctor or an engineer. They wanted to have fun with me, but they would not marry me because in my field the financial prospects were not that good. Most of the Chinese girls who were foreign students came from well-to-do families in China.

"Sonia and I used to meet in church, and then we would go out for coffee. It was not a romantic attachment at first. We went together for two years. Then Sonia got a job offer in Africa. At that time, I realized that I would lose her unless I married her. Sonia is a fine woman. I would miss her fine qualities. She is a good companion. Eventually you do not need a lover. You need a companion." Sonia and Kenneth have been married for 26 years now.

On Lily's (Case No. 40) part, she made every effort to marry within her own ethnic group. She said, "I always tried to be more serious about Chinese boys because that is what Mother wanted me to bring home. I liked that they were smart. Chinese boys that I dated were very athletic. The first fellow I went with was a terrific basketball player. Because I lived in California, they ran the entire gamut. Some of them were very cute. I could bring them home. I would not get a hassle."

Lily had second thoughts, however, when her boyfriend's father had a stroke. His sister went East to help her mother, but her boyfriend said, "I need room to develop." "It didn't seem right to me," said Lily. "In this sense, I was more Chinese than he. He clearly wanted his career to be the most important. I don't know if this is true, but I have a different person as husband."

Lily's next boyfriend was a Chinese doctor. "He had the same feelings. He wanted his dinner on the table. My husband, a WASP, believes the family is most important. When his father was ill, he visited him every day. I would have expected this more of a Chinese male than a Western man. Whatever I do, he will support it, as long as it is not based on a whim . . . . Part of our development together is heavily oriented toward the women's liberation movement. He is very supportive of my activities."

Vivian (Case No. 32) voiced the same preference for a Chinese mate, but it also did not work out that way. "My husband, Bryant, and I used to study together. I was having problems in my chemical engineering courses and Bryant helped me. For six months, that was all there was to it. No romantic attraction. I was seeing a Chinese boy at the time. I would have preferred Chinese boys from a social acceptability standpoint. In terms of dealing with my parents, it would have been easier on them. But Bryant was easy to be with. I felt comfortable with him. He's good-looking. We became friends.

"I remember two Chinese fellows in college who were too stuck on themselves. They felt they were a prize, a trophy. You know how in Chinese society, the male is such a prize. I liked them, but I had to say no. This is the type of person to whom I would have had to keep proving how deserving I was of him."

From the above accounts, one gets the impression that a strong inclination is to mate with one's own kind, but other factors intrude into the picture. Although we may have an idea of the person whom we would like to marry, there are factors beyond the personal that influence or affect the likelihood of mixed marriages, such as the lack of Chinese persons of the opposite sex or the presence of comfortable companions close by. Some structural factors include migration, population size, proximity, sex ratio, family orientation, ethnic insulation, acculturation, social distance and tradition.

MIGRATION

It goes without saying that if the Chinese had not migrated to the United States or if some Americans had not gone to China, intermarriage would not have occurred. Migration, therefore, is a major factor leading to interracial unions. Prior to 1965, Chinese immigration to the United States was inconsequential. Exclusion laws operated against them until 1943, at which time they were given an annual quota of 105. That rate was tantamount to exclusion.

After 1965, Chinese immigration increased dramatically. The immigration act of that year increased China's quota to 20,000, and persons of Chinese extraction emigrating from other countries like Indonesia or Canada would come under the quota of their country of origin, not under the Chinese quota as before. Ethnically, however, these immigrants identified themselves as Chinese, not Indonesian or Canadian. Moreover, in 1980, Taiwan was given a separate quota of 20,000, and in 1983, the Hong Kong quota increased from 600 to 5,000 and after 1987 to 6,000. Ethnic Chinese have also formed a major portion of Vietnamese refugees admitted to the United States. Altogether, the number of Chinese in this country has increased considerably. In 1980, the census counted 812,000 Chinese. The projection for 1990 is 1.3 million, and by the turn of the century it will be 1.7 million (Gardner, Robey and Smith, 1985). For New York City, which is a preferred destination for Chinese immigrants, the estimated Chinese population for 1987 exceeds 300,000, up from 126,000 counted in 1980 (City Planning Commission, 1986).

Immigration remains at a high level. Table 13 shows immigrants admitted to the United States from China, Taiwan and Hong Kong for the years since 1980.

TABLE 13

CHINESE IMMIGRATION TO THE UNITED STATES FROM CHINA, TAIWAN AND HONG KONG, 1980–1985

Year	China	Taiwan	Hong Kong	Total
1980	27,651[a]	—	3,860	31,511
1981	25,803[a]	—	4,055	29,858
1982	27,100	9,884	4,971	41,955
1983	25,777	16,698	5,948	48,423
1984	23,363	12,478	5,465	41,306
1985	24,787	14,895	5,171	44,853
1986	25,106	13,424	5,021	43,551
1987	25,800	11,900	4,706	42,406
1988	28,717	9,670	8,546	46,933

Note: [a] Includes Taiwan

Source: Immigration and Naturalization Service, *Statistical Yearbooks.*

The dilemma men and women removed from their people through travel or migration face is that they may not be able to find mates of their race or nationality in their new surroundings, or the choices may be extremely limited. The alternative is to look beyond one's own group in spite of deterrents or barriers.

Yung Wing, mentioned in Chapter 1 as one of the very first Chinese to come to the United States in 1847 and who later became a diplomat, did not marry until the age of 47. He had come to the United States when he was 18, attended the Monson Academy in Massachusetts and went on to graduate from Yale. Later, he persuaded the Emperor of China to send contingents of Chinese students to the United States, and he was the commissioner in charge of these students. Having spent so many years of his life in this country, he was an American in outlook and values. He had even forgotten his mother tongue and had to relearn it when he went to China. Is it any wonder that he would not accept a Chinese wife with whom he had nothing in common (Lee, 1971)?

There were no Chinese American women to speak of in those days. Eventually, Yung Wing found an American wife, Mary Louisa Kellogg, of Hartford, Connecticut. They were married on February 24, 1875. Despite his personal popularity, his educational background and his high position in the Chinese government, the marriage was not looked upon with favor by New Englanders. Nor did it help his career with the Chinese government. His marriage and his conversion to Christianity brought him under critical suspicion in China (Wing, 1972).

POPULATION SIZE

Each year, close to 50,000 Chinese from China, Taiwan and Hong Kong are admitted to the United States, adding to the size of the population already here. As mentioned previously, these numbers do not take into account those from Vietnam and other countries of Southeast Asia, the Caribbean, Latin America or Canada. One hypothesis regarding exogamy is that the larger the ethnic population, the lower the rate of intermarriage. Part of the reason is in the mathematical calculation. Besanceney (1965) pointed out that each additional intermarriage for a small group results in a larger increase in its intermarriage rate than an additional intermarriage in a large group. For example, in Yung Wing's time, the Chinese intermarriage rate in Connecticut was 100 percent. The second factor is also best illustrated by Yung Wing. There were no Chinese women in Connecticut for him to choose from. As the group gains in size, the choices are greater from within one's own ethnic group.

The laments from many of the interviewees were the limited choices of prospective mates who were Chinese:

> We grew up in Chicago. The parents wanted their kids to marry Chinese, but it was more a matter of demographics. There were no other Chinese around.

> There were no Chinese guys with me in high school. I had no contact with Chinese people at all when growing up. Only time I remember Chinese people is when my parents took us to the Chinese engineers' picnic.

> The only time I saw a Chinese girl was when my parents took me to Chinatown.

The larger the ethnic group, particularly an immigrant generation one, the more pervasive and stronger the ethnic institutions and traditions. More social activities which bring the young people together, are organized by ethnic groups and more social control is exerted over them. This theory has been propounded since 1880 when the census showed that Irish in New York City, where the population was large, married out at a much lower rate than Irish in St. Louis, where their numbers were small (Barron, 1946). Romanzo Adams (1937), based upon his study of intermarriage in Hawaii, formulated one hypothesis of intermarriage: there is an inverse relationship between the size of the group and the rate of intermarriage. His data showed that a large proportion of the few Chinese immigrants in Hawaii before 1852 married Hawaiians, whereas for each succeeding decade afterwards, with the influx of Chinese immigrants, the rate of intermarriage declined, despite the fact that the population had become more native born. He qualified his hypothesis with the statement that this relates to the past and is not to be taken as a forecast.

In a more recent study of Puerto Ricans in New York City, Fitzpatrick and Gurak (1979) said, "Group size emerges as a major determinant of group differences in exogamy rates in general and intermarriage rates with non-Hispanics in particular." They noted that the intermarriage rate for Puerto Ricans was considerably lower than that for other Hispanics, whose numbers were considerably fewer. However, some groups with a strong sense of ethnic identity managed to buck this tendency. Milton Barron (1946), in his book *People Who Intermarry*, talked about the Jews in Derby, Connecticut. In spite of the fact that there were only ten to fifteen Jewish families in town, there was no case of intermarriage involving Jews in 1930 and only one in 1940.

If increased group size decreases the intermarriage rate, then such rates should decline for the Chinese. This is already in evidence in the Kitano, *et al.*, (1984) study of the Chinese and Koreans in Los Angeles and Hawaii. For Koreans in Los Angeles the rates dropped from 34 percent in 1977 to 28 percent in 1979. For Chinese, the rates dropped from 50 percent in 1977 to 41 percent in 1979 (*See*, Table 3). In Hawaii, the Chinese intermarriage rate by marriage declined from 79 percent in 1970 to 76 percent in 1980 (*See*, Table 4). In New York City, the rates remained the same from 1972 to 1982 despite a doubling of the Chinese population (*See*, Table 1). The Chinese in New York City seem to resist exogamy to a greater extent than those elsewhere in the United States. Although the rates are declining, the actual number of intermarriages is increasing.

PROXIMITY

Sue May and Melvin (Case No. 2) lived across the hall from one another in a big apartment complex. Like most urban dwellers, they were nodding acquaintances, greeting each other with a "Good morning" or "Good night" when they met in the hallway or elevator. Before long, Melvin began to watch for Sue May when she left or returned to her apartment. He noticed that she was a cat lover and he had a pet cat himself. Their cats became the opening gambit to their romance.

Physical proximity tends to bring people together. In going through the marriage license applications in the data collection process, this researcher noted that the addresses for brides and grooms were frequently the same. In this day and age, however, it could not be ascertained whether the couple already shared an apartment or whether they merely lived in the same apartment building where there may have been tens or hundreds of apartments.

A university setting provides the most fertile soil for love to bloom. The students are thrown into daily contact over a protracted period of time. They come together in a liberal social atmosphere where family influence is reduced and students are on an equal footing. If it is a campus town, the students are insulated to interact with one another. The educated tend to be less prejudiced and more adventuresome.

Nonetheless, one of the Chinese interviewees met her husband while vacationing in Bermuda. Another met her husband in Kenya where she had gone on temporary assignment in her job. Cupid usually operates best within short distances, but his arrow can still pierce from afar.

SEX RATIO

It goes without saying that eight males cannot pair off matrimonially with one female, and that was the sex ratio among Chinese in New York City in 1930. Where the sex ratio is grossly unbalanced, it is logical to assume that outmarriage would be a solution. Yet, of 254 marriages involving Chinese for the eight years 1931 to 1938, only 26 percent of the Chinese grooms took non-Chinese brides, and no Chinese bride married out (Schwartz, 1951). The excess males either endured bachelorhood or married women in China, knowing full well that they would have to leave their wives behind when they returned to the United States, for the 1924 Immigration Act prohibited Asian men from bringing their wives into this country.

Today, the Chinese sex ratio in New York City is tipped the other way, with more females in the marriageable age cohorts. However, imbalance in the sex ratio does not seem to increase the rate of intermarriage to any appreciable extent. Table 14 provides a breakdown by sex and age.

For Chinese in New York City, 19 years and under and 35 years and over, there are more males than females. For those between the ages of 20 and 34, there are more females. This age category is precisely the one in which most marriages take place. If the age categories are staggered because men usually marry wives younger than themselves, a more accurate sex ratio is derived. For example, if the sex ratio is calculated with males 30–34 and females 25–29,

TABLE 14
CHINESE IN NEW YORK CITY BY SEX, AGE, SEX RATIO, 1980

Age	Male	Female	Sex Ratio
19 and under	18,863	17,490	108
20–24	5,532	5,735	96
25–29	6,271	6,593	95
30–34	5,994	6,105	98
35–39	3,701	3,457	107
40–44	4,203	3,833	110
45–49	4,040	3,610	112
50 and over	15,295	14,042	109

Source: U.S. Census.

the ratio is 91. For males 35–39 and females 30–34, the ratio is 61, or 61 males for every 100 females. In other words, there are 39 excess females in this category, yet in 1982, only 16 percent of Chinese brides married out compared to 15 percent for Chinese grooms. Obviously the gross imbalance in sex ratios has little effect on the intermarriage rate. However, the excess females over males in the most marriagable age category bears watching and may be a factor toward increased intermarriage in the future.

A FAMILY ORIENTED PEOPLE

The Chinese tend to be less family oriented. Fifty-nine percent of both males and females age 15 and over are married, compared to only 51 percent of all males and 42 percent of all females for the city as a whole. The percentages of Chinese single or never married are 35 percent for Chinese males and 28 percent for Chinese females in comparison with 37 percent and 31 percent respectively for the city population (See, Table 15).

The question is whether the propensity toward family establishment will propel the Chinese into intermarriage when mates of the same ethnicity are not available. The dread of a daughter remaining a spinster or a son a bachelor may offset the distaste of outmarriage for some parents who might otherwise oppose such a union.

TABLE 15

MARITAL STATUS OF THE CHINESE, 15 YEARS AND OVER
IN NEW YORK CITY, 1980

	Male	Female
Single	35%	28%
Married	59	59
Separated	1	1
Widowed	3	10
Divorced	2	2
Total	100	100
N =	(50,561)	(48,460)

Source: U.S. Census.

ETHNIC INSULATION

It is almost self-evident that residents within an ethnic community would have a lower intermarriage rate, especially with the Chinese in New York where there are large viable Chinatowns. The residents are more recent immigrants. They are in close proximity with other Chinese. They have a stronger ethnic identity and are imbued with more Chinese traditions and ways of thinking. Community control is greater against those who might wish to marry outside the group. Table 16 shows clearly that Chinatown or satellite Chinatown residents have appreciably lower intermarriage rates than those more dispersed throughout the city. The impact is especially strong on the females. For example, in 1972, only 7 percent of Chinese females residing in Manhattan's Chinatown married out compared to 23 percent for those in other parts of Manhattan. In 1982, the disparity was even greater: 4 percent versus 28 percent. In the outer boroughs where the Chinese population is scattered, the intermarriage rate is considerably higher.

SOCIAL DISTANCE

In a survey of high school students conducted by Milton Barron in 1942, the respondents were asked to list the order of racial, religious or national groups whom they would least like to marry. Blacks headed the list; the Chinese were second. The social distance between whites and Chinese was far apart. Exclusion laws were still in force, severely curtailing their entry into the country. In states like Mississippi, they had been segregated from white

TABLE 16

INTERMARRIAGE RATE BY RESIDENCE FOR CHINESE IN NEW YORK,
1972 AND 1982

	1972		1982	
Residence	Groom	Bride	Groom	Bride
Manhattan	25%	23%	19%	28%
Chinatown	18	7	10	4
Queens	22	26	22	26
Chinatown	12	15	12	15
Brooklyn	30	24	14	17
Bronx	31	30	29	30
Staten Island	36	40	31	27

Source: New York City Marriage License Applications.

schools. In fifteen states of the Union, miscegenation laws made it illegal for Asians to marry whites. The few Chinese in this country mainly operated laundries and restaurants, and there was little contact between the races. Residential segregation and restrictive covenants made sure that Chinese were confined to ethnic enclaves.

World War II brought about drastic social change. Wartime conditions drew people out of their narrow confines and threw them together. Racial barriers were lowered. Ethnic consciousness was raised. People no longer felt they had to abandon their own identities to melt into the American cauldron. The Civil Rights Act of 1964 was finally enacted after prolonged filibustering in the Senate. Affirmative Action followed, opening the doors to minorities in the workplaces and colleges. The Immigration Act of 1965 brought in newcomers with money, education and skills. Negative images of racial minorities moderated, especially those toward Asians. In fact, the negative images were replaced by positive stereotypes depicting Asians as "model minorities," highly educated, hard working, well-behaved, family oriented and well-off. Asians became socially tolerated if not completely accepted into the inner circles. In one instance, when one of our interviewees, a Chinese woman, was marrying into a socially prominent and distinquished family, the grandmother of the groom asked, "Do they mind if we are not Chinese?"

The new generations of Asians, especially those in the marriageable age cohorts, know little of the flagrant discrimination suffered by their forbears in the past. They live in an improved social climate more accepting of ethnic differences. The social distance between groups has lessened, enabling the marrying pair to accept each other and society to better accept the Chinese.

ACCULTURATION

In his assimilation model, Milton Gordon (1964) listed seven progressive stages toward assimilation. The first is cultural or the change of cultural patterns to those of the host society. The second is the structural or the large-scale entrance into cliques, clubs and institutions of the host society. The next step is marital assimilation or intermarriage. Then identificational, attitudinal, behavioral and civic assimilation will follow. This means the eradication of prejudice and discrimination. Gordon's theory is: "Once structural assimilation has been assured, either simultaneously with or subsequent to acculturation, all of the other types of assimilation will follow." His contention is that intermarriage will inevitably follow structural assimilation.

"I never thought of myself as Chinese," said Warren (Case No. 5). "I grew up in suburban Chicago. There were no other Chinese around. My parents came from Beijing and Manchuria, so we did not mix with the Cantonese Chinese. My parents came in the 1940s for schooling. My grandparents and my great grandparents had also come to the United States for their educations, so American values and American behavior have come down to me through the generations. My parents wanted us children to become Americanized. They never taught us Chinese. I felt very self-conscious when I dated a Chinese girl. It never occurred to me that marrying a non-Chinese was out of the ordinary. The first time it hit me was when we told my wife's parents we wanted to get married. They were hysterical. Their reactions jolted me."

Warren, who is a psychiatrist, continued, "Our marriage is very successful because my wife's and my backgrounds are quite similar. We agree on the same things. We think alike. She is more Chinese in behavior than I am. Basically, I am American. I am not like the Chinese from China or Taiwan."

Sylvia (Case No. 13) put it this way: "When I was dating a Caucasian boyfriend, I felt more accepted in American culture because it is dominated by whites. When I was going with Asians, I felt more conspicuous because we were the only Asians in the group. Whether true or not, I thought that way. Given my current awareness of the Asian American experience, I realize that's bad, but when I was younger, I felt like that." Sylvia married a classmate of Scotish/English background. She grew up in Malaysia in a very Chinese household, but she attended English schools. "My Chineseness was already diluted," she explained.

Nelson (Case No. 34) is a *sansei* (third generation) Japanese American. Helen is a third generation Chinese American. They kept insisting that theirs was not an intermarriage. Nelson feels that he is more Chinese than Japanese because he works in Chinatown. What's Japanese about him? "Not much," says Helen. He can't speak Japanese, but he can speak some Chinese. He cooks some Japanese food, but more often he cooks Chinese food. He looks Japanese though." Does he have any Japanese values? "I'm not sure what they are," Nelson replied. "When I went to Japan I didn't feel comfortable at all. I didn't fit in. I felt much more comfortable in Hong Kong." Nelson says he is American first, Chinese second and Japanese third. Both Helen and Nelson were brought up in California.

Joseph (Case No. 43) is a bioengineer married to Linda, who is of Russian Jewish descent. She is third generation of parents who are both medical doctors. Joseph was born and brought up in Newark, New Jersey. Did he ever date Chinese girls? "No, there were no Chinese girls in Newark. I had no car. I had no contact with any Chinese community while I was growing up. It's not that I didn't find Chinese girls attractive. Mainly, I couldn't find any Chinese girls.

"I have always been confused about my identity," Joseph continued. "My parents were very Chinese in their gut feelings, but they were not articulate. Neither of my parents was verbal. There were no stories, no language, no underlying values. I always thought of myself as non-Chinese." Joseph and his wife met in a Tai-Chi class. She was attracted to him because he is an "un-Chinese Chinese." "Culturally he doesn't come across as a Chinese person," she explained.

Most of the above cases illustrate how some people have already internalized American cultural norms and even think of themselves as wholly American. Their families may have had long contact with the United States, so that their Asian culture has been permeated with Western ideas. They may have had no contact with other Chinese and were isolated from the ethnic community. Their roots may go back into American soil several generations, and generation has been found to have a strong correlation with outmarriage, or they may have a preference for American ways over their Chinese upbringing. It is not just that the Chinese culture is diffused by Americanization. The traffic runs both ways. In our case interviews, it was already brought out that the non-Chinese spouses had an Asian bent. They were fascinated with things Oriental. The romances of five out of the fifty case interviews blossomed in China, Taiwan or Hong Kong, and four of these were actually married overseas. The non-Chinese spouses had gone there to study, to teach or on government missions. Four more case interviews revealed that the non-Chinese spouse was in a Chinese American setting and thereby exposed to increased interaction with Chinese people. The Jewish girl who took Tai-Chi classes, the German/Irish student who majored in East Asian Studies, the Japanese social worker who worked in Chinatown are examples.

For these people, their American upbringing had been diffused with exposure to Chinese ways and they must have been favorably disposed.

Within all cultures, there are desirable traits and undesirable ones. However, what is desirable or undesirable is in the eyes of the beholder. What may appear exotic and exciting to one may be strange and overwhelming to another. For example, Chinese boys complain that Chinese girls are too demure. "It's hard to keep the conversation going for an entire evening," they say. All the girls do is nod their heads or respond in monosyllables.

The Chinese girls have their complaints. They say, "Chinese boys are too serious. You date once or twice, and they already have their minds on marriage." This characteristic is an attraction to some non-Chinese women who feel that most men are not willing to make a committment. Chinese girls find their own kind dull and monotonous. "All we do on a date is eat dinner and go to a movie. There's no variety." How about skiing, sailing, going to a museum? "Forget it. Chinese men don't want to do those things." Are they romantic? "In their own way. They just grab you and kiss you without leading up to a romantic mood. After a few dates, you become 'their girl' and they become very possessive." On the other hand, to non-Chinese women, Chinese men are steadfast and reliable. They are family-oriented and will hold down good jobs. Although there is some grain of truth in these stereotypic impressions, they are not applicable to every Chinese person. However, the negative stereotypes tend to strongly influence mate selection outside the Chinese fold.

SOLUTION TO IMMIGRATION STATUS

Legalization of immigration status is a big problem for many students, visitors or business people who come into the United States on nonimmigrant visas. After their original intended mission is accomplished, they are supposed to leave the country. For example, students come to the United States for higher education. A Ph.D. or M.D. degree may take five to six years to complete, after which time they may feel completely at home in this country and want to remain. Yet, if those on a nonimmigrant visa do not depart, they become illegal aliens and are subject to deportation. Some may be tempted to seek a quick solution by marrying a U.S. citizen or a person with the right of permanent residence. This entitles a spouse to the immediate right to stay in this country.

It was said that seamen, who jump ship or are on shore leave in the country, often use this method to effect legalization of their status. Therefore, in the data collection process, special attention was paid to see if seamen were prone to marry out. However, we found no Chinese seaman taking a non-Chinese bride. Of five Chinese women out of the fifty interviewed, two frankly admitted that immigration status was a major factor in their decision to intermarry and three said it was one of the factors. Two Chinese men also said that a chance to live in the United States was a strong factor in their decision to intermarry. In all seven cases, except for the two women who admitted that securing immigration status was a major motive, the marriages are genuine and strong. The other two had already broken up.

TRADITION

For centuries, in many areas of the world, marriage was too serious a matter to entrust to the individuals involved. Mates were selected for offspring by the parents, whose decisions were based more on practical considerations like similarities in class, caste, religion, income, family name, dowry, bride price, or progeny to carry on the family name. It was highly unlikely that parents would betroth their children to someone outside their own ethnic or religious group.

Negotiations were carried on between families, and the prospective bride and groom were seldom consulted, if at all. Under these circumstances, young people did not have to concern themselves about their future mates. One would be secured for them eventually. Family arranged marriages are still quite common with the Chinese in China and even with Chinese Americans to this day. As a result, the whole body of courtship ritual and behavior is nonexistent in Chinese culture. Western concepts are adopted, but they are unfamiliar and alien. To find a prospective mate, to get to know that person through the dating game, to make a judgment and choose wisely are tempestuous and sometimes agonizing steps that the young people go through. And not having precedents to follow makes it that much more difficult.

As has been mentioned several times, young people have been ingrained with the thought they should marry one of their own. Even those who outmarried initially looked for someone in their own ethnic group. Yet when they became romantically involved with a person more suitable to their own needs, they went against their inclinations. Cupid does play a role in today's marital coupling. Nevertheless, even when young men and women think they are choosing mates on the basis of personal attraction or love, they have already been strongly buffeted in their marital choice by factors such as migration, size of the ethnic population, proximity, sex ratio, family orientation, residence in an ethnic community, social distance, desire to stay in the United States, extent of acculturation and strength of tradition.

5

When a Chicken Marries a Duck

M r. Woon, utterly opposed to his son's intermarriage, would repeatedly say, "A chicken does not marry a duck." To him, Chinese and non-Chinese were entirely different species. His arguments: The duck's habitat is the water; a chicken would drown in the pond. A duck could live on land, but to deny its inherent characteristic of being an aquatic bird would go against its nature and affect its whole being. The chicken and duck cannot mate in spite of the fact that both are fowl. These comparisons went on and on, and they do sound logical and convincing if Chinese were analogous to chickens and non-Chinese to ducks.

There is no denying that intermarriage between two races as diverse as Caucasian or black with Chinese would pose special problems in the relationship, especially in one as close and intimate as husband and wife. Differences in physical features, values, religion, expectations, customs and traditions can create misunderstanding, conflict and trouble. The purpose of this chapter is to examine the spousal relationship and some of the major areas of difference to see if they create problems. If so, how do the couples deal with the differences? How are the dissimilarities surmounted? Are intermarriages less stable due to the differences or more exciting due to the injection of novelty and change?

PHYSICAL FEATURES

The man may be attracted to the girl because she is petite, olive-skinned and exotic looking. The woman is attracted to the man because he is tall, muscular and fair skinned. These physical features fulfill the expectations of the couple involved, but other people simply are not accustomed to associating husband and wife of different races. The couple becomes an object of uninvited attention wherever they go. Sam and Kun-yi (Case 29) remember how they used to deal with the stares by playing a game that would embarrass the gawkers. If they passed people going in the opposite direction whom they could surmise were dying of curiosity but were hesitant to stare openly, Sam and Kun-yi would count "One, two, three" and turn around abruptly. Often, the gawkers would have turned around for a second look. Caught in the act, they would be flustered and embarrassed.

When Kun-yi attended Chinese functions with her husband, she was frequently asked, "Didn't your husband come?" Even when she said yes, and Sam was standing right next to her, the questioner would look around the room, expecting to see a Chinese man.

Sorry, I can't go with you. My wife is picking me up in a little while," Chi-yuan (Case 40) told his friends. A moment later, Ann drove up in the car and Chi-yuan ran off. His friends' eyes popped wide open. "His wife!" they exclaimed in disbelief. Their curiosity piqued, they telephoned his home later and Ann took the call. She spoke fluent Mandarin, having taught in Taiwan for several years. That is where she had met and married Chi-yuan. The next time the friends saw Chi-yuan, they teased, "Cheating on your wife, eh? That was your paramour. We know your wife is Chinese. We spoke to her on the phone."

One more example will suffice to illustrate some of the common irritations that interracial couples experience. Jade and Tom (Case No. 46) were coming home on the Long Island Railroad. Jade was sitting on the aisle seat, so when the conductor came around, she handed him two tickets. He punched the tickets. Then he looked straight at Tom and said, "Tickets, please." Knowing that Jade had given the conductor the tickets, Tom paid no attention. The conductor, somewhat impatient by now, repeated his request, "Tickets, please." Whereupon Jade said, "I gave you the tickets." Pointing to Tom, the conductor said, "But he didn't give me a ticket." "He's my husband, and I gave you two tickets for us," said Jade emphatically. That statement caused everyone to turn their heads and stare at the Chinese and black couple.

Even though societies no longer live in geographic or social isolation, marriage is most common between partners who are more similar than different. In intermarriage and departure from this longstanding practice, homogenity is shattered and new conditions are encountered for which new cultural rules must be devised. Because exogamy has only recently become more widespread, the marital relationship will be faced with a set of special problems. Already mentioned was how to deal with the physical disparity when outsiders are not conditioned to accepting interracial couples.

In instances when they were together, Kun-yi and Sam (Case 29) made a game of dealing with curious gawkers. At other times, Sam simply refused to attend Chinese functions where he did not know most of the people. Many of the couples interviewed said that they often left their spouses home when there was any possibility of discomfort in appearing together. One could see that this was the most common method of coping. Husband or wife simply did not accompany the spouse in situations where discomfort would be encountered. Jason (Case 11) a civic leader in Chinatown, always appeared alone at the many social functions he attended. Most people thought he was a bachelor, but he has been married to Carmen, a Puerto Rican, for 21 years. Why doesn't she come with Jason? "Because she feels uncomfortable. There's no major acceptance of her ethnicity. It's hard to quantify that . . . . There was no overt problem, but there was her sense of that." Yet when asked if he ever dated Chinese girls before his marriage, he said, "No, I'm too American."

Do physical differences intrude into the personal relationship? In general, most interviewees said no, at least not on the conscious level in their daily activities. They viewed their mates in their roles as husband or wife. Only few off-hand remarks were made by the wives about the hairiness and body odor of non-Chinese men. Caucasian and black men, as a rule, are physically bigger than Chinese men. They may have hair all over their bodies, whereas Chinese men do not. Caucasians and blacks tend to have strong body odors. Chinese women are less buxom than Caucasian or black women. Differences in skin color, physique and hair color and texture tend to sink into the background in the spousal relationship.

COMMUNICATION

"Marriage demands that partners communicate their thoughts and feelings to one another, and the first of the major problem areas for intercultural marriage is that of communication" (Markoff, 1977:51). The most obvious channel, of course, is language, and when there is no common tongue between the marital partners, the channels of communication are blocked. Fortunately, most of the couples interviewed in this study were highly conversant in English, except for two Chinese husbands from Taiwan. In these two instances, the wives spoke fluent Mandarin, so language was not a barrier. In fact, many of the Chinese spouses who were American born did not speak Chinese at all. Many of the couples were bilingual and even trilingual. For example, the Chinese husband married to the Swedish wife spoke Chinese, English and Swedish. Another Chinese husband married to a Brazilian wife spoke Chinese, English and Portuguese.

Language did not pose a problem with the couples in this study, for most were highly educated. Still, speaking and understanding an acquired language does not mean one can fully express oneself. Take this quote from a young lady who discovered a whole new father when she learned how to speak Chinese, and she regrets having misjudged him.

> My father's English is very good, so it never occurred to me that he was not entirely comfortable speaking it. It wasn't until I started learning a foreign language that I realized that it is possible to be fluent in a

language while still feeling restrictions. When I speak Chinese, even though I can always get my meaning across, I never feel like I am fully expressing myself and my true personality. I believe that my father must have felt many of the same restrictions, for when I spoke Chinese with him I discovered he had a personality that I never knew was there. First of all, I discovered he had a sense of humor, which was something he had not mastered in English. He was much more spontaneous and direct in his replies when he spoke in Chinese. I sensed also that he was more relaxed. It's strange, but until I spoke Chinese with him it had never occurred to me that his reticence might be an aspect of the language barrier. I thought he was just not interested in talking to me, or that he had a boring personality.

Even though one understands the words of a language being spoken, there are nuances of meaning that can only be fathomed by cultural context. Take, for example, the following scenario where a non-Chinese wife had taken great pains to prepare an elaborate meal for her Chinese husband's colleagues. After the last course was served, the husband stood up and said, "Please excuse the poor food that we have served you tonight." If the wife were not attuned to Chinese etiquette, she might have been very angry at her husband. Didn't she slave over a hot stove all day to prepare what she considered a marvelous repast only to have her husband denigrate what she had accomplished in front of the guests?

Chinese etiquette calls for this statement by the host and no one pays attention to its literal meaning. It is just like the response, "Fine," to the greeting, "How are you?" The answer is usually, "Fine," even if you've just had a run-in with your boss, your son just dented the front end of the car and your sinuses are acting up. No one expects you to relate your troubles.

In American culture, people are candid and forthright. They say what is on their minds in a straightforward manner. Yes means yes and no means no most of the time. In Asian cultures, great attention is paid to "saving face." People are reluctant to say no to requests, so they resort to circuitous ways of getting around situations.

Discerning when a yes means yes, maybe or no is a culturally developed skill that basic understanding of the language does not necessarily convey. Misunderstandings may result. These incidents happen in other cultures as well, but they seem to be more frequent in Chinese interactions. American born Chinese, reared in this country, are not as keenly attuned to Chinese nuances, so are often objects of derision by their parents or the China born as uncouth and overly direct in their dealings with other people. For them, these nuances do not pose communication barriers with a spouse also reared in this country.

Peter (Case 23), of Lebanese descent, likes to say what is on his mind. His Chinese wife says, "Peter is too blunt. I'm trying to civilize him." Chinese, especially those reared in China, do not readily reveal their true thoughts or opinions. To someone not attuned to this character trait, it is extremely aggravating when another person refuses to commit himself or herself. This trait has had extra reenforcement in China under a totalitarian form of government. One could never be sure what was the right attitude or right stance at the moment, so it was safer to say nothing and reveal nothing because tomorrow things might change. The Chinese have never enjoyed a history of free speech like the Americans have. This inhibition, however, can be an impediment to spousal communication. It is annoying for the non-Chinese spouse to be unable to elicit an answer or a decision. It takes extra effort to piece together an opinion in an oblique fashion or to learn to interpret the nonverbal signals over time. Time is one of the keys to this problem. The other is to discern the partner's cultural background for these divergences in customs and traits.

Body language, such as facial expression, gesture, vocal inflection, physical contact, and the way people position themselves in relationship to one another is another form of communication. American culture tends not to emphasize nonverbal communication. Words take precedence. We want offenders to say, "I'm sorry; I apologize," even when actions demonstrate that they are contrite. One wife insisted upon her husband uttering an apology even after he had brought her a cup of tea and stroked her hand. His refusal to put his feelings in words reignited the original fight.

The extent of physical contact in nonverbal communication is an area of wide divergence between the American and Chinese cultures. It is common in American society to kiss acquaintances or hug them in greeting and when saying goodbye. Americans of Latin, Mediterranean or Jewish descent are quite demonstrative in these respects. Embracing, kissing, hugging are routine forms of greeting commonly extended even to new acquaintances and do not convey intimacy or deep affection. The Chinese person is very inhibited about physical contact even with one's own spouse except within the privacy of the bedroom. Kissing, hugging or holding hands in public are alien practices to the Chinese. Not only will he or she not engage in such practices, it is embarrassing and discomforting to even witness such behavior.

It is common practice in this country for the groom to kiss the bride at the end of the wedding ceremony. Many Chinese cannot bring themselves to display this affection in front of the wedding guests. Others do it, but squirm in discomfort.

Misunderstandings arise when the non-Chinese partner interprets such behavior as lack of affection or love. A Puerto Rican husband (Case 27) complained that his Chinese wife would not allow him to put his arms around her in public. A Chinese wife said, "My husband says I don't love him enough. Love in America is very different than in Asian culture. I iron his shirts, fold his clothes. To me, that is one expression of love. To him, it is not. Love is when you sit on his lap and do that, that, that" (making the motions of smooching). The husband's retort was, "I didn't marry you to get a housewife." It is not easy for nondemonstrative partners to overcome their reticence to overt affection. The truth of the matter is, most really enjoy and even crave the warmth and touch, although they might not be able to practice it.

When asked to rate the way they communicate with each other, over half said very good and another quarter said good. When there were problems in the quality of communication, the main impediments were not differences in languages, but differences in the way they think.

VALUES

Values are those ideals or principles that one holds dear and subscribes to. Within a culture, values are handed down from generation to generation and are inculcated into the young at an early age almost subconsciously. Consequently, values are endowed with an aura of truth that makes it more difficult to waiver when values of other cultures are encountered. Since we are socialized to believe that our own ideals are the most worthy of attainment, then our ways must be right and others are wrong. Conflict in values, therefore, can create considerable problems in an intermarriage. At the same time, if the parties can transcend the differences, they might bring about an innovative synthesis combining elements of several cultures.

Individualism is one of the most prized values in American society, whereas collectivism is encouraged in Chinese culture. The collective that is the pillar of Chinese society is the family. Family roles determine how each member of a family should relate to the others, so that each person knows his or her exact place and how he or she should behave. Obligation to the family transcends personal interest. In the United States, this value is reversed. Although these values have been moderated, the cultural vestiges are still strong. Having been exposed to the attraction of individualism in the United States, the intermarried Chinese spouse has already flouted tradition, but the range of family centered customs is vast. Filial piety or honoring one's parents is one of the strongest.

Esther (Case 27) came from Taiwan nine years ago. She met Pierre in college and they have been married eight years. Esther has been experiencing tremendous inner conflict when it comes to the question of how much she is obligated to help her natal family. Esther said, "In the Chinese family, we are not just myself. My brothers, sisters have expectations of me. I feel burdened with the family, but my husband says, 'You don't have to.' According to the American way, I know I don't have to, but being Chinese you feel you have to because you are part of the family.

"With Pierre's parents, you treat them as friends. They don't give you pressure. With my mother and father, they give me a lot of pressure. My sister came to the United States, and I had to provide part of her support for two years. Now my mother is here, and my father wants to come. We have a one bedroom apartment, and we gave her the bedroom while Pierre and I sleep in the living room. My mother and father keep reminding me that they raised me and that I owe them everything. If they don't want you to do things in a certain way, they say, 'We raised you in vain.' Then I feel guilty."

Fortunately, Pierre has been very understanding. His response was, "As long as she feels this responsibility, I'll go along with it. She's my wife. You take the good along with the bad." Obviously Esther longed to have her burden lightened, but then she would feel weighted down by guilt. In a way, her marriage was strengthened by her appreciation of Pierre's acceptance of her dilemma and willingness to share it with her.

The extent of family obligation is one of the major cultural conflicts experienced not only by intermarried couples but also by American born Chinese married to the foreign born, by the acculturated married to the traditional. Heavy family demands can create a tug-of-war between the interests of the spouse versus the interests of the natal family. It was surprising to note, however, that the non-Chinese spouses among the interviewees were fairly cognizant of the strong family values and were willing to assume the obligations without too many objections.

Two cases involving non-Chinese daughters-in-law illustrate how accommodating they were to the strong desires of the Chinese for sons in the marriage. One prayed daily for a son so that her mother-in-law would be pleased and the other promised her Chinese mother-in-law that she would have at least five children.

The accumulation of monetary wealth and material goods seems to top the list in the American scheme of values. On the Chinese scale, money and materialism take lesser ranks to educational status and position, family name and honor, although Americanization is altering that. For example, several Chinese female interviewees emphasized that their husbands were Ph.D.s, and they used the argument to persuade their parents to accept the decision because the men were highly educated.

Most of our interviewees had fairly good incomes, so money was not a pressing concern. Generally, both spouses in these intermarried unions work and each had a paycheck. The Chinese spouses were willing to spend money on helping family members, and the non-Chinese spouses were agreeable to this expense. Conspicuous consumption as a badge of success was not in evidence and could only be surmised in two cases by this researcher when flashy cars, fancy neighborhoods, sumptuous furnishings and designer clothes were highlighted by the respondents. In spite of the lesser emphasis placed upon money as an over-arching value in the Chinese scheme of things, Americanization seems to be working a change in the Chinese American outlook, and money is assuming greater importance in their scale of values.

Education, hard work, thrift were highly regarded values with most of the interviewees, regardless of ethnicity. Already mentioned was the high educational attainment and better-than-average socioeconomic status of the intermarrieds. Hard work must have accompanied these attainments. What is noteworthy, also, is that so many of the the non-Chinese spouses were foreign born or only one generation removed from immigrant status. Therefore, Old Country values from these areas persist to a considerable degree and pose little or no conflict for intermarried couples.

At this point, it must be again pointed out that an intermarriage involving Chinese in this country is often not just a bicultural relationship. The diversity of ethnicity in marital partners makes that clear. In most instances, it is tricultural. If the non-Chinese spouse is Italian, Puerto Rican, Lebanese, Swedish, Yugoslavian, Jewish or Japanese, these cultural backgrounds are also brought into the picture besides the American and Chinese ones. For example, the Chinese husband (Case 12) married to the Yugoslavian wife says, "My wife likes to eat a strong goat cheese, and she likes her wine." Dairy products are not part of the Chinese diet, and the smell and taste of strong cheeses are repugnant to the Chinese palate. Neither is alcohol consumed to any extent except on special occasions. Goat cheese and wine are not typical American fare either.

In some cases, a culture intrudes even when it is not part of the family makeup. A Chinese man married to a Puerto Rican wife (Case 11), lives in a predominantly Jewish neighborhood. Their children's speech is peppered with "Oy-vays," and they asked their father if they could be bar-mitzvahed when they came of age.

A Swedish wife (Case 38) who has been in this country for more than 28 years served a hot port wine, Swedish chocolates and ginger snaps during the interview in her home. Her husband took Swedish lessons and they take their vacation in Sweden every year. The couple has been married 26 years. They make their home in New York City and are totally assimilated into the American way of life with leanings toward the Swedish. "In his old age, my husband is searching for his roots in China and things Chinese," said the wife. "He has taken a very active interest in visiting China and writing about the country." The husband majored in English literature in college. Here is a tricultural marriage successfully integrated.

Dr. Richard Markoff (1977), an intercultural marriage counselor in Hawaii, has observed that the most stable solution to bicultural ambiguity is the asymmetrical one in which one of the marital partners adopts almost entirely or in large part the culture of the other. Interestingly, this observer noted that the non-Chinese spouses tend to lean heavily toward adoption of Chinese ways. They make an effort to learn Chinese phrases, and many are fairly proficient in the Mandarin dialect. They prefer Chinese food. They visit the Chinese relatives more frequently and become interested in Chinese history, art, literature and even medicine. The Japanese husband mentioned earlier felt that he was more Chinese than Japanese. Two Japanese wives of Chinese men are active in Chinatown and have no ties with the Japanese community.

The symmetrical solution is where each partner gives up part of his or her culture and adopts some elements of the spouse's culture with a rough sort of equivalence. The latter is successful when the partners are both rather cosmopolitan, when the cultures are relatively similar, or when the married couple is about equally separated from both sets of collateral relatives.

RELIGION

Ruby Jo Kennedy (1944), in her article "Single or Triple Melting Pot?", theorized that intermarriages in the United States occur more readily across national origin or ethnic lines rather than across religious lines and that the American melting pot will not be one gigantic cauldron but three separate ones labeled "Protestant," "Catholic," and "Jewish." This theory might be applicable to white European ancestry people, but most Chinese would not fit into any of these pots, although Christianity is making headway with some Chinese in this country.

The Chinese believe that religion is more an individual matter than part of one's ethnic identity, so their attitudes toward religions are quite tolerant. Consequently, marrying someone of a different religion is less of an obstacle than marrying someone of a different race or nationality, opposite to that held by Kennedy. In this study, the religious convictions of most of the subjects were weak, except for one Catholic pair and the couple who were followers of Sun Yeung Moon (Case 48). Most did not belong to any formal religious group or were only peripherally involved. Differences in beliefs or rituals posed no problems in the marriages. Only one husband, an Hispanic (Case 27), said that religion was an issue. "Chinese or race didn't matter. I would only marry a Catholic girl." In this case, the Chinese wife had been brought up in the Catholic faith. Chinese spouses were quite willing to go to church or synagogue and to bring their children up in the religion of their mates if it was requested. It was not a soul-wrenching decision for them.

Only one spouse formally converted in our case studies. She was a Chinese woman converted to Judaism (Case 9). Her reason: "My husband wanted me to. I had no previous religion. It was not against my beliefs. I did it for the sake of the family. In Jewish life, religion is part of family life. In order for my children to be Jewish, the mother must be Jewish. I studied under a rabbi before my conversion. My husband is chairman of the board at the synagogue, his childhood temple. He has strong sentimental attachments to it, and he contributes generously to it. I am supportive of his role in the temple. We always go there for the High Holy Days."

Obviously a woman with Chinese features would be quite visible in a Jewish synagogue. She was asked, "Do you feel self-conscious? Are you accepted?"

"At first I felt uncomfortable. I was a curiosity. Now when I go in, the ladies greet me and kiss me."

This same woman takes her two children to Chinese school every Saturday. Her husband and she agree that the children should learn about both cultures.

In another case involving a husband who was born Jewish (Case 35), the mother-in-law asked the Chinese wife to convert, but the husband interjected with, "If she had converted, I would not have married her." In a third case, the Jewish wife had been brought up in a kosher home. Could she expect her Chinese husband to practice her dietary customs and give up pork altogether? It was a fundamental decision that had to be resolved. In the end, she decided not to keep a kosher kitchen. Questions like these do arise in an intermarriage and must be settled. In this case, it was highly unlikely that the Chinese husband would eat purely kosher food, and it would be doubly difficult to cook separately for herself and her husband. The Chinese will not compromise on food, but they are quite tolerant and accepting of other religions and their practices, and people who marry Chinese must be willing to put food habits above other considerations.

There was almost unanimous agreement on the popularity of and preference for Chinese food, although it was not always served regularly in the home. The preparation of Chinese food is more time-consuming and takes greater skill. There was no pattern as to how often it was served or who cooked it. Sometimes the non-Chinese spouses enjoyed the experience of concocting Chinese dishes and took it up as a challenge. In other instances, when the Chinese spouses longed for ethnic fare, they would go into the kitchen and cook it themselves or go to a restaurant. In New York City, they would not have to do without. There are over 2,000 Chinese restaurants. In fact, this was the best coping mechanism for most of the couples and probably resolved any issue over food preference that arose.

CUSTOMS AND TRADITIONS

Customs and traditions are habits adopted by a group and generally agreed upon and adhered to. They are handed down through the generations and may be considered the cohesive forces that bind and give a group identity. Why do Christians put up a Christmas tree? Why are black and orange the colors of Halloween? Why does a bride wear white and mourners wear black in Euro-American culture? In China, the bride wears red and the mourners wear white. In entertaining, the guest of honor sits to the right of the hostess under American rules of etiquette. The Chinese place the guest of honor in the seat facing the door. Rationally, no way is the right way. The customs just evolved and in time became established. Emotionally, it is a another story. Members reared within a culture learn the same standards and, from habit, practice the same things. It is only when they are confronted with another set of standards and have to choose that they usually prefer their own ways and may insist upon them.

Chinese brought up in this country or those who have had extensive exposure to Western ways have already accepted many of the American customs, but may also have incorporated many of the Chinese ways as well. Most Chinese in this country will observe the Christmas traditions of having a tree and exchanging gifts. They want to be married in a church even though they may not be Christians. They may not celebrate any Chinese holidays or festive occasions at all, while coloring and rolling eggs during Easter and waving the flag on the Fourth of July. They were socialized to accept the American norms and to act according to the American patterns. As many of the interviewees mentioned, "We are American in thinking and behavior." Under these circumstances, there is no cultural gap even though the marital partners are from different racial groups.

New York City offers a cosmopolitan environment where ethnic customs different from the dominant ones are accepted and appreciated. Customs and traditions are external expressions of a culture, which the non-Chinese spouse can adopt or perform in an effort to please the in-laws or the mate. For example, a non-Chinese bride (Case 40) got married in red rather than white. In accordance with the traditional Chinese ceremony, she bowed to her in-laws and served them tea with both hands. This gesture won the hearts of her in-laws and their objection to the marriage was lessened.

If husband and wife are willing to indicate their choices and discuss the cultural differences beforehand, problems will be mitigated. It is only when the partners do not know about the other's customs or when they become symbols of a power-play, that cleavages occur. One of the most common sources of conflict in Jewish intermarriages is the debate over having a Christmas tree or lighting a menorah (Goldman, 1987; See, also, Mayer, 1985).

Why not have both, or alternate? It would be an acceptance and appreciation of each other's culture.

Oftentimes, there are habitual behavioral patterns in a culture that are not immediately apparent even to the practitioner. An example is the reluctance in Chinese culture to offer praise for a job well done, for good behavior, for good grades, for encouragement. Henry (Case 45) says Chu-lin is always negative. "She is critical of my work. She doesn't give me moral support. She doesn't praise the children when they bring home a good report card. On the other hand, she is highly critical of them and shames them when they misbehave. I believe in positive reinforcement of good behavior. She believes in discouraging negative behavior." "He's right," Chu-lin concedes, "My mother always put me down. Nothing was ever good enough. That was the way I was brought up. Now I find myself doing the same thing." There are many behavioral traits that may be rooted in one's early socialization. The best solution to a bothersome trait is to bring it to the marital partner's attention, as he or she may not even be aware of it.

EXPECTATIONS

James (Case 35) comes from a closely-knit family. Both his parents are in their late sixties and have rarely been separated from each other for more than a day. They are not demonstrative in their affection for each other, but love and devotion are evident in their everyday activities. They are a conservative and traditional Chinese couple, steady and predictable. Reared in this stable and calm household, James wanted his life to be more exciting. Although he was born in Hong Kong, he was brought to the United States as a child and grew up in Brooklyn where there were few Chinese. James envied his peers who were less constrained and who seemed to be having lots of fun. James had to keep his nose in his books and help his parents in their business after school.

James earned a Ph.D. from Columbia University and married his first wife, Sharon, who gave him plenty of excitement. He was never attracted to Chinese girls because "they were dull. You could almost tell what they are going to say or do. With American girls, there is that sense of discovery . . . something new."

Sharon was not Chinese and therefore, "She was very lively, full of life. The openness, the liberated qualities were things that I liked about Sharon. Yet these are the very qualities that worked against me."

James and Sharon were married for four or five years. They are now divorced. James felt ambivalent. "The openness did me in. I found this quality very attractive. Yet when you settle down, I expected a more traditional role of a wife. I am aware there's a contradiction there. Things that attracted later worked against me."

Subconsciously, James' role model for his wife was his mother. He felt that after marriage, Sharon would devote her life to his welfare and be entirely supportive of him. Sharon felt that the Chinese outlook was too confining. It was pushing back women's development. James confessed that he wanted the excitement and discovery in American girls and that he had rebelled against his family. Yet after the divorce, he found great consolation in his family's moral support and became much closer to his parents, but he could not resolve his dilemma. A second liaison, also with a Caucasian woman, ended in the parties going their separate ways. Now, James is taking time off to reassess his concept of marriage.

External reasons, other than mutual attraction and love, can be the lubricant in the path to the altar. Sue Ling (Case 2) was impressed with Melvin's family background. The names of his ancestors were widely recognizable in business and cinema. They were married on the country estate of his grandmother. "I loved his family," said Sue Ling. "They are 'up' people. I wanted to be part of the dominant culture, the white culture. Marrying white is marrying up into the dominant culture." This marriage lasted two years. It was based on the name and fame of the husband's family and not as much on the personality and compatibility of the couple. In spite of this experience, Sue Ling says that if she marries again, she still wants to marry white. She was brought up in a predominantly white setting. Although her parents were immigrants, they were medical professionals. All four of the parents' offsprings have Ph.D.s and all four married out. Sue Ling has a distinquished career in her own right. In a recent venture, the Chinese community gave her tremendous support, so she has become more conscious of her ethnic identity. "How to become part of the white culture and keep my Chineseness, I don't know. I haven't resolved that question yet," Sue Ling mused.

One couple (Case 49), in particular, struck this writer as mismatched. The wife was a beautiful, young, vivacious girl who had gone through sad experiences during the Cultural Revolution and was determined not to go back to China. Yet her values were very traditional. The husband was an older man, quite unconventional in his lifestyle. Yet they have been married five years. According to the wife, "We talk a lot and do a lot of things together." They do not plan to have children because the husband does not want any. Asked why she married her husband, she replied, "I just wanted a man who would treat me good." Her expectations were met.

GENDER ROLES

Contrary to what this writer presumed to be an area of considerable marital conflict in mixed marriages, gender roles did not prove to be so. When asked, most of the couples said the traditional male/female roles had been neutralized, perhaps by the very act of intermarriage itself. Chinese women, in rejecting Chinese males, believing them to be chauvinistic, found their non-Chinese husbands more willing to share in the household chores and more willing to treat them as equals. Chinese husbands, in taking non-Chinese wives, may have moderated their male dominance outlook and behavior. Economic circumstances also have a hand in altering the traditional gender roles. Since husband and wife in most of the marriages were highly educated and both had jobs outside of the home, the divergence in gender roles narrowed and sometimes overlapped, and in one case reversed, with the husband staying home to take care of the baby and the wife holding down a job.

AGREEMENTS AND DIFFERENCES

One question asked of the couples was: All husbands and wives have arguments at some time or other. In your marriage, what are the arguments about? Are they over money, children, in-laws, religious beliefs, personal habits of your mate, cultural differences, leisure time activities or something else?

Personal habits of mate, by far, outranked the other causes of arguments. Those irritating little things like throwing socks on the floor, not screwing on the toothpaste cap, not calling to say you are going to be late, chewing one's fingernails—these were endless bases for arguments, but these gripes are common in all marriages. Money was the second most common cause and, surprisingly, leisure time activities was the third culprit. Arguments would ensue over whether to play golf or play bridge, to go to the movies or to go to the ball game, to visit relatives or visit friends and the like. These might be labeled minor differences between spouses. Major differences like religious beliefs or cultural differences ranked much lower on the scale of frequency or importance.

Other questions sought to establish the extent of agreement in values between intermarried couples. It was found that husbands and wives generally were in complete or strong agreement in religion, filial obligations toward parents, education, sharing the housework, pooling the family income and putting family welfare before individual interest. They were weakest in agreement on whether the children should be taught Chinese and in attitude toward spending money. The non-Chinese spouses generally are more inclined toward spending and the Chinese spouses generally are more inclined toward saving.

DIVORCE

The questions that come to the fore regarding intermarriage are: Are such marriages less stable? Do they tend to break up? The few and scattered studies conducted on intermarriage among the Chinese outside New York City answer in the affirmative. Yes, such marriages are less stable—considerably more so. The findings from these studies are summarized in Table 17.

Five previous scholars have researched and documented divorce rates for Chinese persons in inmarriages and outmarriages in Los Angeles, Iowa and Hawaii as tabulated in Table 17, although the findings are somewhat outdated. The first column presents the rate of outmarriages. The second column shows divorce rates for inmarriages or Chinese marrying Chinese. A comparison between these rates and those for outmarriages in columns three and four reveals striking differences. In every instance, Chinese males and females who married out divorced at a much higher instance than those who stayed within their own ethnic group. In most cases, outmarriages involving Chinese men are more susceptible to breakup, except in the case of Iowa.

The rates for Chinese in New York are given under the Sung entry in the above table and are calculated by dividing the average number of divorces per year (*See,* Table 18) by the number of new marriages for the year 1982 (*See,* Table 1). If we total the divorces among the intermarried Chinese, we get 431 over a period of six years with an average of 72 per year. In 1982, the closest year for which statistics are available, there were 390 intermarriages involving Chinese. This would work out to a combined divorce rate of 18.5 with a breakdown of 23.8 for Chinese males and 13.9 for Chinese females. In comparison, using the same method of computation, the inmarriage divorce rate was 19.3.

The divorce figures were obtained from forms filed by lawyers when divorces become final. This form, called Certificate of Dissolution of Marriage, is filed with the New York State Department of Health and is mandatory, so the divorce figures are exact. Ethnicity is noted on the form, but the statistics are not published. The only way to obtain the figures was by special request and payment to the State Department of Health for a custom tabulation. Even then, this researcher's request was not granted for the type of information sought. For example, the request for divorce correlated with birthplace was not provided, although data on age and educational level were given. Tables, 18, 19 and 20 are based on information provided by the State Department of Health.

Table 19 shows that approximately two out of five divorcees in outmarriages involving a Chinese have a college education. This follows because those who intermarry are better educated. Almost half of the divorcees, whether inmarried or outmarried, have a high school education.

Table 20 shows there is little difference in the age profiles of the inmarried and outmarried when it comes to divorce. The surprising revelation in this table is the 22 percent of Chinese men in inmarriages who divorce their wives after age fifty.

TABLE 17

DIVORCE RATES FOR IN AND OUTMARRIED CHINESE AMERICANS
(PER 100 POPULATION)

Source Place Date	Divorce Rates		Outmarriage	
	Outmarriage	Inmarriage	Chinese Male	Chinese Female
Barron[1] Los Angeles 1948–1959	4.4 (f) 4.2 (m)	1.4	10.2[a]	7.4[a]
Lind[2] Hawaii 1958–1962	49.2	17.2	25.4	
Monahan[3] Iowa 1944–1967	66.6	6.4	15.6[a]	29.1[a]
Schewertfeger[4] Hawaii 1968–1976	67.0 (f) 69.0 (m)	0.0	18.7	14.1
Tseng[5] Hawaii 1958–1962		18.0	43.0[a]	31.0[a]
Sung New York City 1982	14.0 (f) 13.0 (m)	19.3	23.8	13.9

Note:　[a] Spouse white
Sources: [1] M. Barron, 1972
　　　　 [2] A. Lind, 1964
　　　　 [3] T. Monahan, 1970
　　　　 [4] M. Schewertfeger, 1982
　　　　 [5] W. Tseng, et al., 1977

TABLE 18

DISSOLUTION OF MARRIAGES AMONG THE CHINESE IN NEW YORK, 1981–1986

	NYC	Upstate NY	Total
Chinese Male & Chinese Female	1,238 (74%)	75 (47%)	1,313 (72%)
Chinese Male & Non-Chinese Female	258 (16%)	47 (29%)	305 (17%)
Non-Chinese Male & Chinese Female	173 (10%)	39 (24%)	212 (11%)
Total	1,669 (100%)	161 (100%)	1,830 (100%)

Source: New York State Department of Health.

TABLE 19

EDUCATIONAL LEVEL OF DIVORCEES INVOLVING CHINESE—IN AND OUTMARRIAGES IN NEW YORK STATE, 1981–1986

	Inmarriage				Outmarriage			
	Men		Women		Men		Women	
	No.	Pct.	No.	Pct.	No.	Pct.	No.	Pct.
Not stated	108	8	107	8	29	5	29	5
Elementary	266	20	299	23	57	11	55	11
High School	602	46	639	49	226	44	247	48
College	337	26	268	20	205	40	186	36
Total	1,313	100	1,313	100	517	100	517	100

Note: Data in this table is for New York State.
Source: New York State Department of Health.

Among our 50 case studies, there were six divorces and, in the opinion of this researcher three shaky unions, again close to one in five. However, when the interviewees were asked if they had ever seriously contemplated divorce, only one in ten persons said yes.

TABLE 20

AGE OF DIVORCEES—IN AND OUTMARRIAGES INVOLVING
CHINESE IN NEW YORK STATE, 1981–1986

| | Inmarriage | | | | Outmarriage | | | |
| | Men | | Women | | Men | | Women | |
Age	No.	Pct.	No.	Pct.	No.	Pct.	No.	Pct.
Not Stated	30	2	34	3	4	1	14	3
< 19	1	—	8	1	0	—	5	1
20–24	22	2	82	6	19	4	50	10
25–29	145	11	268	20	82	16	123	24
30–34	304	23	311	24	136	26	129	25
35–39	229	18	226	17	105	20	85	16
40–44	163	12	129	10	65	11	46	9
45–49	137	10	102	8	33	6	29	5
50 plus	282	22	153	11	73	14	36	7
Total	1,313	100	1,313	100	517	100	517	100

Note: Data in this table is for New York State.
Source: New York State Department of Health.

In essence, the New York data show there is practically no difference in marital instability between inmarried or outmarried couples. Inmarried couples divorced at the rate of 19.3, the outmarried at a slightly lower rate of 18.5. These findings are at variance with previous findings and must be viewed in light of today's changing social attitudes toward divorce and causes of the breakups, but spousal differences in the intermarriages do not seem to be a major factor. In the United States, the rate approaches one divorce for every new marriage within a given year. Both Chinese inmarried and outmarried divorce rates are considerably lower at about one in five. These comparable rates reflect either greater acceptance of divorce by inmarried Chinese couples as a solution to marital problems or the possibility that outmarriage is no longer much different from inmarriage. Since this is one of the most recent studies on mixed marriages, more research is called for to probe deeper into the changes that have come about.

CONCLUSION

Since husband and wife choose each other, often over family objections and overwhelming odds, their mutual attraction must be exceptionally strong and their acceptance and tolerance for each other's differences unusually great. The dissimilarity in physical features will subject them to unwelcomed attention. The lines of communication may be obstructed not necessarily because of language differences, although this may be a factor, but also because of cultural differences. These may be more than bicultural, not just involving Chinese and American values and traditions; they may also be tricultural or multicultural. For example, the Chinese man brought up in Indonesia who married a Brazilian but now lives in the United States has a quadricultural background. Jewish American or Puerto Rican American cum Chinese American marriages have the added dimension of religion with which to contend. The tricultural situation seems to be the norm rather than the exception in intermarriages among the Chinese in New York City.

Yet, there seems to be strong agreement among the couples interviewed as to outlook, values, traditions and expectations. Surprisingly, the most common causes of arguments were in the areas of personal habits of the spouse, money and leisure time activities—a situation not unlike that in all marriages.

Although previous studies of Chinese intermarriage in places like Hawaii and Los Angeles showed a much higher rate of divorce in mixed marriages, such was not the case in New York City. The rate of marital breakup among the outmarried seemed to parallel that among the inmarried. In response to the question, "Would you say that your marriage is successful, mildly successful, satisfactory, not very good or complete disaster", 74 percent said successful, 16 percent said mildly successful, 8 percent said satisfactory and 2 percent said it was a complete disaster. As mentioned previously, only 10 percent of the interviewees said that they had ever seriously contemplated divorce.

If the spousal relationship does not seem to be the area of pitfalls in mixed marriages, one must look at other impacting factors such as the parents and family, societal attitudes and sanctions, and offsprings of the union.

6

What Do Father and Mother Say?

Pandemonium broke out in the Wong household when the eldest son announced at the dinner table that he wanted to marry a Caucasian girl. The mother flailed her arms and wailed between screeches and moans. The father roared and thundered, alternately pounding the table so that the dishes jumped and rattled. The sisters cowered in fright because they, too, had been dating white boys. The scene at the intended bride's house was no less traumatic. "Why?" pleaded the parents. "Why a Chinese man?"

Family objection is the biggest hurdle and worst problem that intermarrying couples face. Of the 50 cases interviewed, family objection was raised by the bride or groom's families or both in 34 cases. Family reaction was non-applicable in 9 cases, either because the marrying couple had no families, were older in years, were entering into a second marriage, or were spatially removed from the family. In seven cases, there was little or no objection, but of these seven, only three were pleased or favorably inclined. Negative responses came from all groups, but the most intense hostility emanated from the Chinese and Jewish families.

Why should family objection pose such a formidable problem? Isn't marriage a personal matter between a man and a woman who are attracted to each other and who want to cement the bond in a more permanent union recognized by society and by law? Invariably, response of the young people to their parents is, "I am the one who has to live with him/her, not you." Although they want parental approval or blessing, they feel the parents should have little say in the choice.

In fact, throughout most parts of the world, down through history, until very recent times, marriage was never a choice between two individuals. It was always a family or a clan decision based upon considerations of race, ethnicity, social class, family background, health, wealth, beauty and other factors. Couples were matched to preserve endogamy or inmarriage and homogamy or similarities in background, social class and temperament.

The family, not the person, was the unit of society. Roles within the family were well-defined within cultures. So were the duties and obligations, traditions and rituals, values and beliefs. In return, individuals found emotional, financial and social security within an institution where they had ascribed and immutable places. To preserve familial continuity and to maintain its stability, persons brought within the family fold had to share the same traditions, customs, values and status. To be otherwise was to be disruptive.

An extremely important function of the family was to preserve the culture, the lineage and the ethnic identity of the group through the rearing, training and socialization of the young. Anyone foreign to the established rules, customs, traditions, roles and viewpoints governing behavior would alter the norms and the prevailing ways. Therefore, the decision of selecting a mate was an extremely important family concern and not left to young people. Personal attraction and compatibility between husband and wife were not the primary considerations in the decisionmaking. It was continuity of the family and stability of society.

Of course, the argument is that these conditions no longer govern mate selection in the United States, and functions of a family are quite different today. Expectations from marriage are primarily sexual gratification, emotional support and companionship. Primary interaction is between husband and wife and not intergenerational. Even the function of child rearing has diminished, as evidenced by the declining birth rate and the shrinking size of the household. Bonds between siblings are weak and tenuous and even weaker for aunts, uncles and cousins. Young couples no longer live with their parents or in-laws. Therefore, the choice of a spouse must rest upon considerations other than the traditional ones because the marital relationship has narrowed down to that between husband and wife. Nevertheless, it is important to see why families object so strenuously to intermarriage.

Parents see in their offspring the immortality of themselves. They see a continuity of their flesh and spirit in an unending chain. Someone of a different race or nationality coming into the family breaks this chain. The blood will be altered for future generations. Invariably, ties to the ethnic groups are loosened. Parents sense the act of intermarriage as a rejection of themselves and a refutation of their upbringing. Family bonds may be further shattered if the alien member does not speak the same language and communication lines are blocked.

In the United States, marriage creates a new and separate family. In China, marriage is an extension or continuity of the family line. For example, Carol (Case 23) compared her former Chinese mother-in-law in China with her present American mother-in-law. She said, "When I crossed my first husband's threshold, I became a member of the family. My mother-in-law treated me like her daughter. Whatever she had, I had. I felt I belonged. My present mother-in-law treats me like an outsider. She will not give me anything. If you are married to a Caucasian husband, never expect the family to treat you good, no matter how good you are to them. They will never include you as a member of their family. When they make disparaging remarks, I ignore them. I am married to the man, not to the family."

In documenting family attitude toward intermarriage, statistics may be more convincing and concepts more profound, but actual occurrences highlight the human experience and give us a true sense of how families react when confronted with an intermarriage close to home. This chapter is devoted to case studies of family attitudes toward intermarriage ranging from outright disowning of the offspring to acceptance. Sad to say, most of the cases leaned toward the hostile end. Out of 50 cases interviewed, only three families on both sides were pleased and accepting of the marriage. Most were displeased, but eventually resigned themselves to the situation. Some of the stories are heartbreaking, some heroic. The additional strain demanded stronger marital bonds. Love had to be greater to persist despite family aversion to the union.

The following case studies give concrete examples of what actually happened to couples, how couples dealt with the objections and what were the outcomes. The cases presented are highly representative of those interviewed.

DISOWNED

Kun-yi and Sam

Forty years ago, the scene toward intermarriage was not as favorable as it is today and especially not in China. Kun-yi (Case 29) came from an upper class, well-to-do family in China. She was a college student and somewhat of a rarity because she was one of only three females enrolled in the entire university. That meant she never lacked for beaux. Progressive in outlook and rebellious in nature, she took up the cause for women's rights.

Sam was an American soldier stationed in Kumming in the aftermath of World War II. He and Kun-yi met at a party for G.I.s and dated secretly for about a year. Then they eloped. Kun-yi never told her family about Sam and Sam only recently met Kun-yi's family after 40 years. The family acted as though Kun-yi had blemished the family name and brought shame upon them. All contact was cut off for the first 20 years until she received a letter stating that her uncle was coming to the United States as a diplomatic attache. It took another 20 years before Kun-yi went back to China to visit her brothers and sisters and for them to visit her in New York. The memory of her rejection hung over the reunions. The scars were still there.

Sam's family was no less hostile. He was an only son from a white, Anglo-Saxon Protestant background. When Sam and Kun-yi married, they sent ten registered letters home, none of which were answered or acknowledged. When they returned to New York, the couple had to stay with Sam's parents because of a terrible housing shortage. The in-laws reacted with extreme hostility toward Kun-yi until the newspapers heard about it and published articles on what was happening. The publicity scared the in-laws and they backed off. Still, there was nowhere for the couple to go, so they stayed and suffered. Kun-yi said, "I tried harder to please my American mother-in-law than I would have had to with a Chinese mother-in-law. Eventually my mother-in-law accepted me, but my father-in-law never did—not even to his dying days, and he lived to his nineties."

In this case, Kun-yi was a G.I. bride and the marriage took place over 40 years ago. Attitudes in those days were more hostile toward people who violated the norms. Kun-yi is somewhat bitter against her own family and her in-laws, but the marriage is a highly successful one. She confesses, however, that because of her rejection, she is constantly trying to prove to others that she is not a "bad woman."

Jean and William

"To this day, my mother will not talk to me nor allow me to set foot in her house again, and I have been married for 12 years." William (Case 15) speaks of his estrangement from his mother with great sorrow. He thought that after the birth of his second child he would take his two girls to visit Grandma. Surely the sight of two such adorable girls would melt Grandma's heart, but when he rang the doorbell Grandma answered and slammed the door in their faces. She is adamant. "When he married that girl, he was no longer my son," said Mrs. Chao. Deep down in her heart, she also hurts. Over and over again, she repeats the story of how her son deceived her and how he reneged on his promise. She feels betrayed that her sons have not considered her wishes and that her life's work in bringing up her children has been in vain.

William loves his mother and his heartache is equally painful. But he also loves his wife and they have been very happy together over the years. William's father was equally opposed to the marriage, but he has softened a little. He visits his son's family, but when he gets home, he vents his anger and frustration psychosomatically. Outwardly, he has mended the bridges, but viscerally he becomes emotionally upset.

The family is literally torn apart over their son's outmarriage. The problem has defied the efforts of other family members to bring them together. The parents' anger and rage may have intimidated another son from marrying out, but it may also have intimidated him from marrying at all.

In this case, the son had to make the painful choice between his parents and his wife. He chose the latter and suffers the consequences of rejection from his parents. Heartaches abound for both parents and son in this instance, and no answers are in sight.

Jade and Tom

When Jade and Tom (Case 46) decided to marry, Jade was far from home—Hawaii. She was going to college in New York, where she met Tom. She was already engaged to a Chinese man back home, but she broke the engagement. Her family said, "Come home and let us talk to you one more time. If you choose to go through with it, then you have to understand that we won't have anything to do with you because you have to live with them and live a black life. You won't be Chinese anymore."

"They thought the threat would make me come to my senses," Jade explained, "but they raised me to be non-prejudiced and independent. They would have objected even if my husband were white. I dated someone previously who was white, and they put the pressure on me to break it up. I have been married 32 years now, but for ten years I was disowned. I always wanted to go back to Hawaii, but I was afraid of what my family would do to Tom. Finally I went, but I wrote to them first saying, 'If you don't accept Tom, we'll come on our own, but you're not going to bother him if he comes.'

"It bothered me at first, but I am very strong. I discovered I didn't have a great need for my family, but I wasn't completely cut off. My brothers and sisters, uncles and aunts came to New York, and they visited and told me the family news. My parents have come to accept the kids. One daughter went out to Hawaii and lived with them for a while. My father now asks, 'Why don't my grandchildren come to visit me more often?'"

When Tom's mother was first told, she said she would have preferred that her son marry a black, but that he could do what he wanted. After the marriage, Jade said her mother-in- law was extremely supportive. "She took care of the kids when they were young and I went out to work."

In this case, Jade was far removed in physical distance from her natal family anyway, so the impact of her emotional severance was cushioned somewhat. On the other hand, her mother-in-law's acceptance gave her moral support.

DISAPPROVAL

Charlene and Simon

Sometimes the pressure is too much to bear, so you wait and do nothing, hoping that the passage of time will solve the problem. For Charlene and Simon (Case 22), it took 25 years. The groom's mother of German Catholic background opposed her son's marriage to a Chinese woman. "No," she said, and her will was so strong that her son dared not oppose her until she died 25 years later. Even then, when the wedding took place, the groom's brothers did not attend. When one hears about these heartrending stories, one is inclined to wonder in awe about the patience and strong bonds of love to surmount such obstacles.

Melody and Irving

Irving and Melody (Case 9) did not wait 25 years, but they did wait eight years. The delay was due in part to the groom's mother's objection that the bride was not Jewish. It was not that Melody was Chinese; anyone not Jewish was unacceptable. She was opposed to the marriage to the very day of the wedding. Irving was even loathe to bring up the subject with his mother. It always ended in an argument. She made terrible scenes. She was especially concerned about what her friends would say. She gave Melody the cold shoulder even though Melody was studying with a rabbi in preparation for her conversion to Judaism.

Irving's sister, however, loved Melody. It was his sister who finally convinced the mother to attend the wedding and not make a scene. When Irving's mother gave her consent, she said, "Okay, you can get married, but don't have children together." In this respect, Irving and Melody disobeyed her as well. When they had their first child, the new grandma did not react much to the event. When the second child was brought to Grandma, she held it close and remarked, "This is the happiest day of my life."

Family objections to the marriage of Irving and Melody were not entirely on Irving's side. Here is how Melody put it: "I wanted to please my father, but at the same time I wanted to rebel. That's why I couldn't bring myself to tell my father that I wanted to marry a Jewish guy. He had notions that Americans weren't family oriented. They just wanted to fool around. He didn't think I could have a good marriage. My parents are still in Taiwan."

A common way of dealing with likely family objection is not to tell, thereby postponing the day of reckoning. This recourse is possible when the parents are not in the United States, but it entails manuevering and secrecy and probably a big dose of guilt feelings.

Sylvia and Murray

Sylvia (Case 13) is a petite Chinese girl from Malaysia who met her husband, Murray, at Princeton University. Now they are doing post-graduate work at Cornell University, and have been married five years. "We simply did not tell my family," said Sylvia. "I knew the reaction would be negative. I didn't let my family know until I was compelled by circumstances. Otherwise, I would have postponed it indefinitely.

"After we graduated from Princeton, Murray and I got teaching positions at the University of Malaysia for three years, so the question came up of how to break the news to my family. We thought it was easier by letter and then a visit. Upon receiving the letter, my father called long distance and said if I came with my husband, don't expect him to be home. My mother said she was not happy, but since the deed was done, she would accept it. After this call, Murray and I went to Malaysia. Although the physical distance separating my family and us was not far, we did not visit my parents until a year later."

When the young couple finally called upon Sylvia's parents, the reception was cool and uncomfortable. The parents could not speak English and Murray could not speak Chinese, so they said very little to one another. The couple was not even invited to stay for dinner, so they drank their cups of tea and left. Sylvia remarked, "My father didn't leave the house, as he threatened to do, but he continues to act as if I were not married. He didn't tell any of our family friends or relatives about my marriage."

"I felt very uncomfortable and very angry. My father is a traditional Chinese.I never felt very close to him, but then I have been away from home for such a long time. He is a businessman and only has a grade school education." Murray's reaction: "Sylvia and I discussed this beforehand and we knew what would happen. I understand. We accept each other (the parents), but we are apart. My parents took the news better than I thought. My brothers and sisters knew I was going with Sylvia, so it wasn't news to them."

Flora and Seth

In her own words, Flora (Case 20) told about her family's objection to her outmarriage. "I didn't tell anyone that my first husband and I had broken up. I got away with it for years because he worked in a different town. I continued to send out the Christmas cards with both our names, so when I decided to marry Seth, I didn't tell my family either. We went to City Hall. To this day (eight years later), I have never told my aunts and uncles outright. My parents are dead now, and my brothers and sisters know, but they do not like it."

Flora and Seth are both in their mid-fifties, and Flora and her siblings are American born Chinese. Yet the siblings have very conservative ideas about divorce and intermarriage. "Only within the last three years have my brothers and sisters accepted our marriage, but we have been married eight years already," said Flora. "How do they express their disapproval? They don't come to our social functions when invited. They don't show up at the family

Chinese New Year's celebration if they think Seth will be there. They don't invite us to family weddings. My sister's daughter is getting married. They invited me, but did not invite Seth. I spoke to my sister over the telephone, and I get the feeling that they would be embarrassed if we attended, so we are not going. I used to get quite upset. It took me a couple of years to get over the rejection."

The fact of the matter is, Flora never got over the ostracism. In her next breath, she says she likes her niece and very much wishes to attend the wedding. She is in a quandry about what to do. If she does not go, she will feel left out and harbor deep resentment. If she goes by herself, Seth will feel hurt and she doesn't want to give her relatives that satisfaction. If she goes with Seth, they might cause him discomfort and his presence might cast a pall over a happy occasion. What to do?

On Seth's side, his 80-year-old mother said the best thing that ever happened to her son is Flora. He was 46 years old at the time, and his mother just wanted him to get married. Seth maintains that the couple is included in his family events, but Flora does not feel comfortable there. He defends her feelings by saying, "She doesn't have to go if she doesn't want to. She doesn't have to prove anything with them. I know how she feels because her sisters keep telling her they don't feel comfortable with me either."

DISPLEASED BUT RESIGNED

Vivian and John

"I went to Vivian's (Case 32) father and asked his permission to marry his daughter," said John, whose ancestry reaches back on his mother's side to the Daughters of the American Revolution and on his father's side to an uncle who was a state governor. Vivian's father is president of his family association in New York's Chinatown, a graduate of the University of Chicago and a court interpreter. "He gave me permission," said John, "but I could see he was not pleased."

Vivian took up where John left off. She sat down and talked to her father. "Father, it's not as if John were a sailor or a waiter. He's a gentleman. He's a Princeton graduate. He's an engineer. You know I have gone with this Chinese fellow and that Chinese guy, and I wouldn't have them on a silver platter. John and I get along fine." For a moment, the father's feelings would be soothed, but as Vivian continued, "Occasionally you will see the pain on his face. It's like a thorn that surfaces, and he will say, 'But he's not Chinese.'

"It's his friends," explained Vivian, "and I'd like to punch them in the nose. They keep commenting, 'You have only one daughter. How come you let her marry an American?' Then father is pained. My mother? She just said, 'You're

25 now. You should get married.' My mother is much more understanding. She is a social worker and has a Masters degree from Barnard College."

What was the reaction from John's family? "Vivian charmed the socks off my father, but he did caution me to give it more thought, even though I come from a liberal family that never differentiated between black and white, men and women. My father told me to consider how my marriage would impact upon my career, and what would happen if I were transferred to the Deep South or Midwest where people viewed intermarriage in a different light." John laughed after this statement, "Because," he said, "in the petrochemical company that I work for now, 20 to 30 percent of the engineers are Asians and one of my superiors is Asian."

Rose and Francis

This is Rose's (Case 10) story: "My father died when I was three months old, so my mother raised me all by herself. She did bead work and embroidery at home, so she was always available; she was always there. She is a strong woman and I am just like her. I was brought up in New York's Chinatown. There weren't that many Chinese around at that time—about five to ten Chinese kids in each class where we went to public school. The rest were Italians and they always called us 'chinks.' I got into a lot of fights with them. The principal would then send for my mother."

Rose went on to college where she earned a B.A. and then to graduate school where she earned a Masters degree in health administration. But she never lost her scrappiness. She was an activist during the period of campus unrest of the 1970s. "My mother didn't like the people I associated with, and I resented her control over my life. I rebelled. We tortured each other, but I could not walk away from her. I would have a guilt trip just leaving her by herself.

"One day I brought home a black guy. She took one look and walked out of the house. She didn't speak to me for three months. She would walk past me and heave a great sigh. No conversation. That bothered me a lot. It was a real hard time. I wanted to leave but she said, 'If you leave, you are no longer my daughter. As far as I am concerned, you are dead. That's it.' That was the worst. I gave up the black guy although he was going to Howard University and he came from one of the best families in St. Croix.

"My husband, Francis, is white. I told my cousin, who is having trouble with his family now because he wants to marry an Italian girl, 'You should have brought home a black girl first. Then your family would be happy and relieved that you are marrying an Italian girl.' Maybe that's why my mother did not object as much to Francis. Now mother loves Francis dearly. His relationship with her is better than with his own mother. Yet, when he picks her up in Chinatown with the car and her friends asked, 'Who is that?,' she will say, 'A friend,' not her son-in-law." Rose and Francis have been married for nine years. They have a little boy.

Rose's relations with Francis' Irish/Catholic family did not improve with time. Francis has an M.B.A., but the rest of the family are not well-educated. According to Rose, "They are bigots. Francis does not have those values. He is a maverick." When Francis' parents came to visit the couple, they expressed surprise that black and white kids were playing together in the streets. To the parents, that was a neighborhood drawback. To Rose and Francis, that was a plus. Nevertheless, when Francis' mother went to the hospital and the father was left alone and helpless, Rose invited him to stay at their house. None of his own children wanted to do that.

In these displeased but resigned cases, the parents are ambivalent. They wish the marriages weren't so, but since they can do little about it, they try to make the best of the situation. Most parents whom this writer has known and observed are deeply pained. As some of these interviewees intimated, the parents try to cover up and not admit the outmarriage to their friends and relatives. In fact, they even try to deny it to themselves. The in-laws may seem to get along, but deep down inside they are unhappy. Take the case of a family friend who celebrated both of her children's weddings in a lavish manner. Hundreds of guests attended and the parents were all smiles in the reception line. One would assume acceptance by the parents when they throw banquets on such a grand scale. Subsequently, the mother confided to this writer her frustration and unhappiness over her children's outmarriages. Her pride in being Chinese was intense, and she interpreted her children's outmarriage as a rejection of the parents. Surface relations with her son-in-law and daughter-in-law are cordial, but below the surface anger and frustrations fester. Once, in reference to her grandchildren, she remarked, "Those are not my grandchildren. They are little foreign devils."

ACCEPTANCE

Lucie and Jack

"My parents were absolutely delighted," replied Lucie (Case 26), a tiny wisp of a young woman who can boast a Masters of Fine Arts from Harvard University. I was the first of my four brothers and sisters to get married and two more married out afterwards. My mother wishes for a Chinese daughter-in-law, but that's not going to happen because my brother is dating a non-Chinese girl.

"To my parents, my husband Jack is perfect in every way. He's a Harvard graduate, a vice-president of a computer software company. He's stable, hard-working and smart but not nerdy. In a funny sort of way, he's Asian in his modesty. He's kind of square. Very handsome. We're both from Catholic families, but we are not very religious. In fact, Jack has been a bridge for me to my own family."

Lucie's upbringing is almost entirely American. She was brought up in the northern suburbs of New York. "My parents never tried to put us in a Chinese setting. I had no contacts with Chinese people at all when growing up. The only time I remember being with Chinese people was when my parents took us to the annual Chinese engineers' picnic. There were no Chinese guys with me in high school. I once dated this Chinese guy. It was awkward. That was the only Chinese guy I ever dated.

"My father is a college professor and my mother is a school teacher. They both came from China. How about my in-laws? I think the shock had worn off by the time we got married. Jack used to date other Asian girls. They saw me as being good for their son. I taught him to dance. I got him to talk more and warm up a lot. They think I am reliable, I have a good education, and they think I am a class up from them. Jack's mother said, 'I never have to worry about Jack with Lucie.' The more distant relatives raise their eyebrows though. They don't know what to make of me. I am accepted in spite of the fact that I am Chinese because I am an intellectual. I write short stories that have been published and Jack's parents proudly display them on the coffee table. They are proud of their son, too. He's the only one in the family who has been to college and Harvard to boot!" In this case, the husband's family thought their son had gained status by marrying into an intellectual family.

Ann and Chi-yuan

"When the invitations were sent out, our friends and relatives could see that I was marrying an American girl," said Chi-yuan (Case 40). My father's colleagues at the bank in Taiwan all accepted the invitation to the banquet. Ordinarily they just send a 'hung-bao' (red envelope containing gift money), but this time they wanted to see the American lady who was marrying my father's son. My father felt very good about that. He felt that he had gained status and face."

Ching Li and Frank

Mother Helms was thrilled with Ching Li (Case 33) from the very moment that Frank brought her home. "Treat him gently," she entreated Ching Li. He was burnt (romantically) when he was 20 years old and he hasn't dated since. I've been so concerned that he would never be interested in women again." The couple now live with Frank's parents and you couldn't find a happier more close-knit family. They simply radiate with joy, especially now that Ching Li is pregnant.

Mother Helms did not have to convince Ching Li very much. Frank was already head over heels in love. The couple have been married for over two years. The way they look at each other, one would think they are honeymooners. The extended family consists of Frank's parents, his younger sister and the young couple. They have a small wing of the house to themselves. Mother Helms would make the perfect model for a Norman Rockwell picture. She was baking bread and pies when this writer visited. Father Helms, sitting in the kitchen, completed the domestic scene.

They simply love Ching Li, especially Father Helms whom Ching Li spoils with her massages and acupressures to the temple. Sister is a big tease; Ching Li still has a hard time differentiating between what is a joke and what isn't. But one can see that Ching Li is treated like a princess.

Ching Li is from Taiwan. She met Frank in college. He is majoring in East Asian Studies in preparation for a career in the Foreign Service. He offered to tutor her in economics if she would tutor him in Chinese. Ching Li has been in this country for only three years, so she is still unsure of American ways. For example, if she got up late in the morning, she would feel somewhat uneasy. When Mother Helms greeted her with a "Good morning," Ching Li wasn't sure whether her mother-in-law was being facetious that her daughter-in-law did not rise early or whether she was really sincere in her greetings. Frank kept reassuring her that his mother meant well, but Ching Li was uncertain. She imagined that her mother-in-law was pressuring her to have a son and was displeased because she was not pregnant after two years.

Ching Li was transferring the Chinese cultural expectations to her American family, but her suspicions were unfounded. "I know now I was looking for bones in an egg," she said. "My mother-in-law is such a nice woman. She is simple and pure. I am the only one among her four daughters-in-law who lives with her and sits and chats with her. My father-in-law is a carbon copy of Frank. I cannot ask for better."

Ching Li's parents are in Taiwan, but they are just as pleased as the Helms. Frank is fluent in Mandarin and probably knows more about Chinese history and culture than most Chinese. They converse on the telephone and have no problem communicating.

The above case studies run the gamut from out-and-out rejection to warm reception. All three cases of acceptance were presented. The remaining cases were non-applicables or varying degrees of rejection, mostly in the displeased but resigned category. With the overwhelming majority of Chinese families, a son-in-law or daughter-in-law who was non-Chinese met with opposition to some extent, but the degree of opposition varied with the person's race or ethnicity. There was less opposition to someone who was white or Asian, although residual dislike of Japanese from World War II was evident. The greatest hostility was directed against blacks. Non-Chinese families had their scale of opposition based just as much on race and ethnicity as well, but Chinese people seem to have gained social status in recent years because of their educational attainment and economic mobility. As such, a Chinese son- or daughter-in-law meets with less opposition than it would have years ago.

Undoubtedly the emotional anguish and energy spent on dealing with parental objection puts a heavy strain on the marriage. One can perhaps surmise that many would-be intermarriages knuckled under intense family pressure. These cases are the ones that persisted. In most instances, opposition was more intense from the Chinese side of the family. Parents with better educations were more likely to be accepting, but this was not always the case. Parental preference was for a son- or daughter-in-law of Chinese extraction. However, but parents also discovered that they have very little say in the matter. Their helplessness only aggravated their frustration.

How did the couples cope? It was quite evident that many postponed marriage until they were absolutely sure of their feelings for each other. Fortunately, for many in our study, the in-laws were overseas or spatially removed so that contact was occasional or rare. Some kept their marriages a secret, knowing that to reveal would create an unpleasant scene and perhaps a family rift that might not heal. Some were cast out, disowned or cut off outright. Invariably, there was a deep sense of guilt and conflict between respect for the parents and love for the spouse. As was stated at the beginning of this chapter, family objection was the most troublesome issue for intermarried couples.

7

Stares and Sneers

When two people are strongly attracted to one another and are deeply in love, they tend to block out the world around them and have eyes only for each other. They see their relationship as a personal one, impacting only upon themselves and not subject to control or interference by outsiders. They even resent parental intrusion. Yet, from the preceding chapter, it was evident that the families of the couple strongly affected the lives of the intermarried, even when they could not prevent the union altogether. In fact, family objection was the most troublesome problem in intermarriage, according to the respondents interviewed.

Even outsiders, with no connections or ties to the intermarrying pair, will have their say. In fact, society or the community at large has always exerted its control over the institution of marriage, for "the aims and desires of the individual do not always coincide with those of society at large. Certain laws and regulations may well serve the best interests of society while at the same time restricting the freedom of specific individuals or groups" (Kephart, 1977:14). Thus, to marry, one must obtain a license. To divorce, one must obtain a court decree. There are laws regulating who may marry whom—for example, the proscription of close relatives or the insane from marrying.

In most regions of the world, intermarriage is frowned upon, discouraged and even outlawed. Twenty states in this country had miscegenation laws that made interracial marriages illegal. Fourteen of these prohibited marriage between whites and Asians (Kephart,1977; Sung, 1967). Most of these states were in the West and the South; New York was not one of them. The laws varied from state to state. Some merely declared such marriages null and void and offspring of the union illegitimate. Others subjected the pair to fines and jail terms. Still others punished the minister or official who conducted the marriage ceremony.

Miscegenation means mismatching of people or mongrelization of races. It was a disparaging term reflecting the disdain in which intermarriage was held. These laws were enforced vigorously in the South, especially against black men who would marry white women. It was not until 1967 that these laws were declared unconstitutional. Although the laws have been struck down, American society has not come around to full acceptance of mixed marriages.

Just as some states were completely intolerant of interracial marriages, others were quite liberal and accepting. Hawaii has always been cited as an example of harmonious racial amalgamation, but according to the respondents from Hawaii in this study, strong prejudice remains. The data for this study is taken from New York City, where the population is diverse. As headquarters for the United Nations, representatives from 110 nations converge in this city. The city is the premier commercial and trading center and the crossroads of the world. In New York City's public schools, over a hundred ethnic groups or nationalities are represented. The schools integrate the children of these diverse peoples, so that differences in physical features, languages, customs and outlooks are encountered daily. With such mingling, there should be greater tolerance for and acceptance of intermarriages. There is. Responses from our interviewees indicate fairly wide-spread social acceptance of Chinese married to whites. Chinese-black unions still encounter unpleasant experiences. Unfortunately, the Chinese community seems to be less tolerant than the larger society at present. Responding to the question, "When you announced your pending marriage to your friends, what was their initial reaction: disbelief? some reservation? complete acceptance? other? (describe)," almost three out of four said complete acceptance, but one out of five said disbelief or reservation. Two persons said shock or hostility.

The next question asked was: "Have any friends disassociated themselves from you since your marriage?" Nine out of ten said no.

In response to the question: "How would you rate the extent of societal acceptance of your marriage?" four out of five said it makes no differences. Others mentioned odd looks and stares. Sometimes there are nasty remarks or avoidance. Additional comments to this question repeatedly stressed that disparaging looks or remarks usually occurred in Chinatown.

As reported by our interviewees, societal reaction ranged from the very mild to the more extreme measures. Many were isolated incidents. However, they were vividly etched in the minds of the respondents, so that they could not help but impact upon the thinking and behavior of the couples.

STARES

Almost all the persons interviewed experienced stares or double-takes when in public with their mates. The couple would attract attention wherever they went, especially if their physical features were markedly different. Of course, the Chinese stand out anyway, but if the spouse has blonde or red hair, the contrast is even more striking.

One respondent wanted to dismiss the stares with these words: "Sometimes, we read too deeply into people's motivation. An intermarriage is an anomaly, and anytime you have an anomaly, that creates a fascination. There's a difference between fascination and prejudice. It's uncomfortable to be stared at, pointed out or viewed with special scrutiny, but I try to give people the benefit of the doubt." However, another man was not as magnanimous. His experience was that the Chinese gawk the most, so whenever he and his Chinese wife became the target of unwanted attention, he yelled out, "What are you staring at?" The question voiced in Chinese by a non-Chinese always rattled the gawkers, shifting the discomfort to them.

UNCOMPLIMENTARY REMARKS

These can be jeers or sneers as the couple is walking by. When some Chinese men see a Chinese girl with a non-Chinese companion, they may shout, "What has he got that we Chinese don't have?" If it is a Chinese man with a non-Chinese woman, they may assume the girl is low class or a prostitute. In Singapore, where Sylvia (Case 13) had gone with her husband to teach at the university, people would yell, "You Chinese girl. What are you doing with this red-headed devil?" "I was hurt," Sylvia recalls. "Here I was, a university professor and Ph.D. and I was taken for a loose woman."

Becky's (Case 1) Chinese coworkers bluntly said to her face, "It won't last because he's American. "Their taunting made me want to put my husband in the closet [hide him]. I didn't want people to know that I was married to him. We were very close at first. We did everything together. We wouldn't even take a walk separately. My coworkers kept saying that John was bad. They said, 'If he's American, more chance that he will be bad.' That influenced my mind. I had to put him in the closet." The remarks did affect the marriage. Instead of doing things together as they did in the beginning, Becky tried to avoid being seen with John. A divorce is now pending.

RUDENESS

Rose (Case 10) relates her experience: "When we were first dating, I would not go to a Chinese restaurant. This was in the 1970s. People would stare at us and give us dirty, evil looks. They looked at me as if I were a whore, a tramp. The waiters would sling the food at us. It was terrible. They don't do that any more. I never got that reaction in a non-Chinese setting. As a result, I avoid Chinatown."

People are unable to or refuse to grasp the fact that two people from different racial backgrounds can be married. On a tour to Niagara Falls, other passengers kept intimating to Calvert that Yi-fong (Case 21) was just a girl he was taking on an extramarital fling. Although he introduced Yi-fong as his wife, they kept referring to her as his girlfriend and made snide remarks about his leaving his wife at home. Calvert and Yi-fong had to endure the snickering innuendos for the entire trip, which ruined their vacation to a large degree.

SOCIAL LIFE

According to Melody, (Case 9), "Friends do not involve you in social activities as much. Social life for me is a little difficult. Irving doesn't feel it as much because he is in the office so much. I don't have many friends, but I did have a group of close friends. After I got married, many of my Chinese friends did not feel comfortable with Irving. They have to speak English when he is around. They don't want to exclude him, so the conversation is constrained. If I were married to a Chinese husband and living in this house, my friends would be 99 percent Chinese. We would be invited out more often on weekends. We are not invited because of Irving. It's not because they don't like him, they just don't have as much fun. They can't include him in the conversation."

After seven years of marriage, Melody feels estranged from her Chinese friends. She is going to great lengths to make friends with her neighbors primarily for the sake of her children, but the fact that she has to try so hard says something about her social acceptance in the affluent neighborhood in which they live.

In coping with social acceptance, intermarrieds tend to make friends with people like themselves. For example, one couple, a Chinese husband with his German-born wife (Case 48)—matched and married by the Rev. Sun Yeung Moon in one of his mass weddings—socialize primarily with couples like themselves. They live in church-owned quarters and interact with many interracially married couples. These couples did not choose their mates. Because of their religious beliefs, they are firmly convinced that their marriages were ordained by God through the offices of the Rev. Moon. Since they live in a tightly knit community of like-minded people, they accept the divine guidance of Rev. Moon and follow his teachings.

Among our interviewees, there were artists, poets, writers and filmmakers. The social circle of these people consists of creative nonconformists who are more tolerant and more accepting of racial differences. A number are in academia. These people work in a liberal environment and experience little, if any, social ostracism. In fact, social rejection by the larger society is not that much of an issue in New York for most respondents. In other parts of the United States, it can be different.

FEAR

Long-time residents of the metropolitan area, Joe and Linda (Case 43) were totally unprepared for what happened to them in Georgia. For their honeymoon, Joe and Linda decided to rent a trailer van and drive south through the eastern coastal states to Florida. Joe is Chinese American, born and brought up in New Jersey. Linda is Russian/Jewish American, born and brought up in Connecticut. Now both live and work in New York City. As they drove through Georgia, Joe became apprehensive and alarmed. He described it this way: "They didn't do anything to us. It was more a feeling and a look, but at times, I really feared for my life. The knowledge was that we should be careful about being affectionate and demonstrative toward each other. No, it was not a question of my being Chinese; it was us together, Linda and me. Especially if they thought we were more than friends. We didn't even go into a hotel. I was afraid. There was a lurking fear that there might be violence directed against us. We have no interest in going there again."

A more exasperating story is told by Wei-Min (Case 31), born in China but more a citizen of the world, since her parents were in the diplomatic service. She had lived in countries throughout the world and was married to a Spaniard. Wei-Min was an urbane, sophisticated woman who had traveled extensively and who could anticipate unusual situations that might arise from country to country.

When she went to China in the late 1970s, she made reservations in advance, specifying a double room for herself and her husband. Checking into the "People's Hotel" in Sian, the room clerk gave them separate rooms. Thinking it was a mistake by the desk clerk, she reiterated her request for a double room and showed them her hotel confirmation. "You cannot share a room with a white man," the clerk retorted.

"But he is my husband," Wei-Min responded. She had come prepared and she whipped out her marriage license. The desk clerk disdained even to look at the document. "I don't read English," she said, and no amount of arguing could dissuade her. This happened not once but two more times in other cities of China. One desk clerk explained her actions. "I'm trying to take care of you," she said.

"I'm a grown woman. Not even my mother has to take care of me," groaned Wei-Min. "They viewed me as a loose woman trying to make it with a white man. I had thought about living in China when I retire. Now I am not sure. Maybe if you live there and people get to know you, it will be different." That, Wei-Min knows very well, is highly unlikely.

OVERCOMPENSATION

Kun-yi (Case 29) sensed that the Chinese did not accept her, and she wanted so much to be accepted, so she had to make an extra effort to be nice. When she married Sam in China forty years ago, she had to keep the marriage secret at first. If the military found out, they would have shipped Sam out and the couple would have been separated. He could even have been court martialed and dishonorably discharged. The U.S. government discouraged its soldiers from taking war brides in foreign countries and did everything to prevent such marriages. Since Kun-yi lived with Sam, though married in fact, she was called a foreign prostitute.

"Chinese feel that women who married Americans are not decent. This is a stereotype. For me, that hurt a lot because I feel that I had to prove my character. How do I prove it? By helping others, by doing volunteer work in the Chinese community, by giving." Kun-yi is now a highly respected member of the Chinese community, but she had to overcompensate to gain this respect.

This overcompensation manifests itself in many ways. For example, this researcher noted that a large number of the most actively involved members in Chinatown in social service or political activism were married to non-Chinese. The connection between community involvement and intermarriage was pointed out to the interviewees and answers were solicited, but the respondents could not explain why this was so. It was not a conscious act on their part. One conjecture is that they had given up some of their ethnic identity and were trying to recapture part of it by working for the community.

KEEP THE MARRIAGE SECRET

Already mentioned are two cases where the parties tried to hide the fact that they were intermarried. In Kun-yi and Sam's (Case 29) case, the concerns were real and consequences severe if it were known. In Becky's case, John (Case 1) became a liability that called for constant justification and constant explanation. It was simpler for her to deny her husband when she was working in Chinatown. "Put him in the closet" were her words.

Chu-lin and Henry (Case 45) work in the same office, but their colleagues do not know they are husband and wife. How they can keep such a secret is hard to comprehend. Chu-lin is an advocate for minority issues, so it would be difficult for her to explain why she married a white man. "I love him," she said, "but I won't go to Chinese restaurants with him, and Henry does not go to Chinese American functions." This has gone on for thirteen years. How does this double life impact upon the marriage? On one hand, it could be a strain. On the other, it could add a hide-and-seek excitement to the relationship (however, a year after the interview, Chu-lin and Henry separated).

LIMITED RESIDENTIAL OPTIONS

Three black/Chinese couples mentioned difficulties in trying to buy a house. In these cases, the husbands are black. "When we were first married," said Jade (Case 46), "we lived in a nice apartment in upper Manhattan. The superintendent was intermarried, too, so he was very nice to us. When we wanted to buy a house, we looked in Brooklyn. They just locked us out. They wouldn't let us come to see the house; didn't want to talk to you. We looked around in Queens and were steered to certain areas by real estate people to places that were changing. We bought in St. Albans where there are some whites, but most of my neighbors are black. I have no trouble being accepted by blacks.

Thelma (Case 36) worked for a governmental agency that fights discrimination. She and Noel live in Manhattan, but when they wanted to buy a summer home in upstate New York, they found that they could not get a mortgage even though they were well-qualified financially. Thelma filed a complaint through her agency and the mortgage came through quickly. They moved into their summer home, but, alas, did not get to enjoy it for long. Shortly afterwards, they received a call in their Manhattan apartment that someone had put a torch to their house.

"Yes," said George and Elizabeth (Case 4), "we anticipated problems buying a house in the suburbs. This is one of the reasons why we are not interested in buying. We agreed that we would live in Manhattan." Elizabeth piped in, "George does not want to live in an all black neighborhood and I don't either. Nor do we want to live in Chinatown."

Several couples mentioned that their mixed marriage was a factor in deciding where to live. Two couples moved into Chinatown. Several mentioned that they deliberately chose a mixed neighborhood so that their children would be more accepted. New York City was fine, but most admitted that they would not move to the South or into a small town where people might be less tolerant.

IMPACT ON EMPLOYMENT

When a company wants to promote a man into a position of importance and responsibility, they also check the qualifications of his wife. Will she be a helpmeet? Will she help promote the image of the company? Will she be a liability? Thus, is marriage to a Chinese a liability?

Bette Bao married Winston Lord, a young diplomat she had met in her world economics class at the Fletcher School of Law and Diplomacy in 1963. Winston was preparing for a career in the Foreign Service with a special interest in the Far East. He was fluent in Chinese. When the couple decided to marry, they were informed of a U.S. State Department ruling governing the careers of foreign service officers with immigrant spouses. "Henceforth, your husband is barred from all work in China," Bette was told. That was devastating news to the newlyweds. Fortunately, the damage was not permanent. Twenty-three years later, in 1986, Winston Lord became American ambassador to China (*Chinatown News*, 1987).

Jade and Tom are well acquainted with discrimination. They attended graduate school together. Jade has always had a professional position, but Tom experienced severe discrimination at the beginning. He wanted to be a salesman, but was shunted into the warehouse. Fortuitous circumstances—the New York public school strike in 1971—opened doors for him. When the regular teachers walked off the job, Tom was asked to take over some classes and he stayed on. Since then, he has risen to the position of school principal. Jade and Tom have been married for 32 years, but they have not had a choice of where to live.

In his book *Gods of War*, John Toland (1985) tells the story of a young American woman, Floss McGlynn, who married a promising Japanese diplomat, Tadashi Toda. As a result of his marriage, Toda was shunted to foreign outposts that rank "closer to prunes than plums." The downgrading came immediately after the wedding ceremony. John Toland is a noted historian whose wife is Japanese. Undoubtedly, he had personal experiences and keen insight into what intermarriage meant for a couple whose countries were at war. Although *Gods of War* is fictional, the book reveals the tensions, the strains, the agony of mistrust from all quarters, where loyalty to one side meant treachery to the other.

An historical case also comes to mind. The story of Yung Wing was mentioned earlier in this book. He was the first Chinese student to come to the United States for his education in 1847, predating by one year the influx of Chinese miners during the California Gold Rush. He was brought here at the age of eighteen by the Rev. Samuel Brown, who enrolled him in the Monson Academy in Massachusetts. Yung Wing went on to graduate from Yale in 1854, whereupon he returned to China and persuaded the emperor to replicate his experience by sending other students to study in the United States. Many of these students eventually made an enormous impact in introducing Western culture and technology to China.

The first contingent of students arrived in 1872 and were headquartered in Hartford, Connecticut. Yung Wing accompanied them as chief commissioner. On February 24, 1875, he married Mary Louisa Kellogg in her parents' home. The Kelloggs were a prominent family in Hartford. Yung Wing was forty-seven years old; Mary Louisa was twenty-five. According to the Rev. Twichell, who married them, Yung Wing had felt that "there was no Chinese woman whom he would marry and no American lady who would marry him" (Lee, 1971). In spite of Yung Wing's personal popularity, his educational background and his high position in the Chinese government, the marriage was not looked upon with favor by New Englanders. Nevertheless, Yung Wing was personally happy in the match. Unfortunately, the marriage only lasted eleven years, ending with Mary Louisa's death. During the marriage, Yung Wing made several trips to China, but Mary Louisa never accompanied him. Two sons were born of the marriage (Yung Wing, 1909).

How was the marriage received in China? According to Prof. C.S. Gu (1984) of Shanghai who authored a book on Yung Wing, communication in those days was very slow. Crossing the Pacific Ocean took four to five months, so it was some time before Peking knew about the marriage. The reaction was unfavorable. The headline of an article that appeared in the *Hartford Courant* (1912) read: "Love Ended 1870 Test of Chinese School Here." The marriage was only one factor in the abolishment of the Educational Mission and the recall of the hundred or more students. Other reasons played more important roles. The discriminatory acts against the Chinese in California and the heavy emphasis upon Western studies to the detriment of their Chinese studies by the students were the primary reasons. Nevertheless, another article in the *Hartford Courant* (1912) read:

> One of the most critical blows leading to premature termination of the mission came as a result of the young leader's own actions.
>
> So determined was he to completely Americanize the young scholars that he let them neglect their Chinese studies which were supposed to parallel their Occidental education.
>
> He converted to Christianity. Then he married Louisa Kellogg, daughter of one of Hartford's leading physicians. All this, coupled with whispered rumors back in China, brought Yung Wing under critical suspicion. The mission suffered under his "tainted" image.

None of the respondents interviewed for this study felt that their marriages affected them adversely in the area of employment. On the contrary, in one case involving a Chinese man from Singapore who was married to a white woman (Case 8), the effect was preferential treatment. When he returned to Singapore with his bride, he was immediately promoted. His wife was given preference in obtaining Singaporean citizenship, which she received speedily, although it was a widely known fact that Singaporean citizenship is very difficult to come by. Contrast this experience to that of

Sylvia (Case 13), a Chinese woman with a white husband in Singapore. She received jeers in spite of her university position.

Obviously a double standard exists in Singapore. Chinese men who marry white women are looked upon as having gained a prize. To the onlooker in the street, seeing a Chinese woman with a white man evokes stereotypes that the woman is a prostitute.

A live-wire Chinese insurance agent (Case 17) said, "All that counts in my company is productivity. As long as I bring in the business, they are not interested in my personal life." Already mentioned was the petroleum engineer who laughed when he was asked whether his marriage to a Chinese woman affected his career mobility. "My immediate superior is Asian," he said, "and so are half the engineers there."

LITERARY ACCOUNTS

A revealing and detailed account of the social status of interracial families is told by James Loewen (1971) in his book *The Mississippi Chinese: Between Black and White*. The Chinese there were once classified as black, but are now reclassified as white as evidenced by the W on their drivers' licenses. In the 1940s, about 20 to 30 percent of the Chinese men married out, predominantly to black women, although some took white and Mexican women as wives even though it was illegal.

From the white perspective, interracial families were black. From the Chinese perspective, such families were to be shunned and the community tried to hide them from public scrutiny. In fact, when a filmmaker tried to seek out some of these families, the Chinese families were incensed. Black attitudes toward black women who married Chinese were no better. They looked upon the women as "uppity," as escapists denying their own ethnicity. As one black woman, married to a Chinese merchant for over 20 years, said, "I'm prejudiced against by three races!" (Loewen, 1971:142).

Men feel the ostracism no less than their wives. The men find better acceptance among blacks, but they do not want to be identified as black. They want to retain their Chinese identity, yet find this road blocked by the Chinese. Offspring of the interracial unions are labeled black in a racist society that recognizes only two colors. Surprisingly, the mixed blood Chinese find closest affinity with light-skinned blacks, themselves undoubtedly the offspring of black/white parentage. As one man put it, "We are a group of people without a race, off to ourselves" (Loewen, 1971:146).

The most gut-wrenching story of an interracial marriage is told by Han Suyin (1965) in her book *A Crippled Tree*. It is the story of her parents' marriage —how they were mesmerized by each other, how Marguerite Denis fought her family and fought convention to marry Yentung Chou. When

Marguerite's father locked her in her room, she kicked a hole through the door and ran off with Yentung who, too, defied his parents' wishes and those of the Chinese Consul General. They thought their love could conquer all. Marguerite was willing to become totally Chinese. She followed her husband to China upon the completion of his higher education, but she had no way of gauging the adjustment that she would be called upon to make. She was despised as one of the hated white race trying to subjugate China. She could not fit into the extended family setup. She was shunned by the foreign community. The French doctor would not even treat her desparately ill son because he was a half-breed. In the end, even Marguerite's indomitable spirit collapsed. She returned to Europe, estranged from her husband and children. Her anguished cry was: "Oh, do not tell me there is no heaven, no paradise for me, for surely I have deserved one, I have had my hell on earth" (p.192).

Yentung tried desparately to make his wife happy, but societal forces were greater than both could deal with. Too many daily occurances rubbed their nerves raw. The realization came one day when he found Marguerite weeping on her bed, her flaming red hair in disarray about her shoulders. It was this red hair that had bewitched him at first and caused him to lose his heart, but now this hair was ugly to him. "I thought, how ugly she is, how repulsive, how foreign! . . . What enchantment had been cast upon me to think her beautiful, and now the spell had gone, and my engrossment revealed for what it was, almost a perversion, an obscenity . . . how could I ever have married such a one?" (p.287).

GUT FEELINGS

No one spoke of physical violence against them and, of course, the law no longer exacts fines or punishment for intermarrying, but even for bystanders the issue can be emotionally charged as expressed in this poem by Eugene Hum Chang titled "Hypnogenocide" (Planas and Chow, 1978):

> Walking down Telegraph
> What's this I see?
> An Asian woman
> With a white man
> Or should I say
> A white man with
> His Asian woman
>
> . . . Deep inside something is released
> It rushes upward, growing
> Pain spread through my body
> I hurt, I hate, I hurt

... I am catapulted into the past
Ugly visions machine-gunning through my mind
... White men killing Vietnamese, Koreans, Japanese
White men killing men like me
White men killing me

We are very close now
She clinging to him
With puppy dog eyes
He, a hyena with his own women
But now, a lion with this woman

Should I strike
First her, then him?
Traitor, traitor
Murderer, murderer.

According to Elaine Kim (1982), who quoted the above poem in her book *Asian American Literature*, "Intermarriage between whites and Asians has been seen in recent times by some Asian Americans as evidence of racial conquest and cultural genocide rather than social acceptance and success for the Asian minority."

Basically, the aversion to intermarriage boils down to fear—fear of the unknown, fear of the stranger, fear of race extinction. The unknown creates uncertainty. This person does not look like us. He or she does not have our values or follow our traditions. Our ways are familiar and comfortable. If someone foreign to our ways comes into our group, our way of life may be changed or modified, and change creates tension.

In some primitive societies, the word for stranger is equivalent to enemy. Either you are one of the tribesmen or you are a stranger, and stranger means enemy (Wood, 1934). There is no middle status between these two opposite relations. A stranger intruding into the territory of another group is put to death primarily because he represents danger or fear of the unknown. No doubt, these fears still reside in modern man. When a stranger penetrates a group in an intimate relationship, the fear is intensified.

One of the primary instincts in human beings is race preservation and, to the same extent, group preservation. The group may be a race, a religion, a nation, a common tongue. Invariably, there are strong propensities to preserving the group. Patriotism and religious fervor exacts the highest sacrifice from those defending their countries or their faiths. We generally think of protecting our country in times of war or of keeping the faith, but what about altering the group from within through intermarriage?

Society's apprehension toward mixed unions is rooted, to a large extent, on the fear of loss of group identity or race extinction. Issue from the marriage will be different from both parental groups. The blood will be diluted, never to run pure again. In spite of such fears, public attitude toward intermarriage has become more tolerant and reaction relatively mild, at least in a cosmopolitan city like New York.

8

New Breed of Americans

Lurking in the minds of most intermarried couples is the concern about offspring of the union. Such children are believed to have problems of identity, not sure of which group they belong to and not fully accepted by either group. The sense of not belonging creates a feeling of alienation and sense of low self-esteem. Societies throughout the world have labeled such offspring in derogatory terms such as half-caste, half-breed, mixed bloods, marginal persons, *hapas* (Hawaiian pidgin meaning half white and half Japanese) *babas* (Malaysian, meaning half Chinese and half Malayan), *mulattos* (Latin American term derived from mule), *mischlings* (Jewish term), mongrels, etc. Han Suyin (1965), herself of mixed parentage, phrased it so vividly in her book *A Crippled Tree*. "A mixed blood. Marguerite's offspring! The way they said it I must have sounded liked excreta . . . ."

There may be differences of opinion between the parents as to which culture the child should be reared in, which religion or tradition the child should adhere to. Physical characteristics may cause other problems. The child may not resemble either the father or mother, causing him or her to feel different and uncertain about his or her identity. These factors may cause personality disorders affecting the child's social behavior.

Yet there are positive assumptions about mixed children as well. The most prevalent, of course, is that mixed marriages bring about a cross-fertilization of the races, which invigorates the blood. The offspring are supposed to be better-looking and healthier in physique. Corollary to this belief is that these children are more intelligent and more creative.

FEWER CHILDREN

Undoubtedly, the negative beliefs seem to outweigh the positive in the minds of intermarried couples because they definitely have fewer children, at least in New York City among the Chinese. A comparison by couples, inmarried and outmarried, shows a significant discrepancy in the number of children they have. According to the 1980 census, (*See*, Table 21) 49 percent of non-Chinese wives married to Chinese husbands had no children at all and 30 percent of Chinese wives who intermarried had none either. Compared to inmarried Chinese families, the percentage with no children was only 15 percent. Outmarried couples consistently had fewer children than the inmarried.

TABLE 21

FERTILITY OF MARRIED WOMEN INVOLVING CHINESE SPOUSE— IN AND OUTMARRIAGE, BY PERCENT, 1980

	Children Ever Born							
	0	1	2	3	4	5	6	7+
Inmarriage	15%	16%	28%	19%	19%	6%	4%	2%
Outmarriage								
Non-Chinese Wife	49	21	16	11	3	0	0	0
Chinese Wife	30	26	20	11	9	3	0	1

Source: U.S. Census Public Use Sample Data.

Data from the intermarried couples interviewed for this study confirm the hypothesis that mixed couples have fewer children. Of the 50 couples interviewed, 18 had no children, 17 had one child, 2 adopted a child, 11 had two children, 1 had three and 1 had seven, for a total of 51 children. That averages out to one child per family. This average would have been smaller if the family of seven children had not tilted the numbers upward.

However, the lower fertility rate for women in mixed marriages cannot be ascribed solely to the factor of intermarriage. Women who are younger and better educated and who have higher status jobs, as is typical of our respondents, do tend to have fewer children. These characteristics may impact as strongly on child-bearing as intermarriage.

Child-rearing in this day and age is difficult enough, but for parents of mixed offspring there are added parental concerns of physical appearance, cultural factors, ethnic identification, siblings who look different, and possible shame or rejection by the offspring.

PARENTAL CONCERNS

Physical Appearance

A child is the product of both parents, so when they are of different racial strains, the offspring is an amalgam of both races, neither totally Chinese nor totally black, Hispanic or Caucasian. The parents do not know what to expect.

As one Caucasian interviewee mentioned, "When my first son was born, he had red hair. I said to the nurse in the hospital, 'This is not my son.' My second son was born with black hair. Now both of them have brown hair. When they are with me, they look more Caucasian. No one would say they are Chinese. When my husband is with them, people will look at him and say, 'That's why.'"

Parents see their offspring as an extension of themselves. It is natural to want the child to look like them. As Eberhard and Waldron (1977) explain:

> For example, a mother-to-be who has discussed the issue of a mixed ethnic child with her husband openly and thinks herself free of ethnic and racial concern may suddenly become extremely worried about the child's looks, the color of his skin, his facial features. A Caucasian mother may ask herself whether she wants to give birth to a child who is not like her, but 'yellow and slant-eyed' like her Oriental husband . . . . The Oriental father may be concerned about how his parents and relatives will react to the racially mixed baby. If the extended family subtly or openly objected to the marriage, a 'different looking child' might increase feelings of resentment of the spouse or the child. If this conflict stays unresolved, the child will experience from the start an ambivalent acceptance which will have damaging effects on his own development of trust and self-esteem.

If the child does not look like the mother, who is the primary caretaker, outsiders may not see the relationship between them and may often mistake the mother for a babysitter or nursemaid. Myra (Case 5), of European extraction, is the wife of a Chinese physician. They have a son who looks "very Oriental." She is constantly asked, when wheeling him in the park, "Whose baby is that?" This annoys her to no end. In another case, no one believes a Chinese grandfather (Case 14) that the red-headed child he is taking care of is his own grandchild, offspring of his daughter who is half white and married to a red-headed Caucasian husband.

When outmarried parents were asked what their children looked like, this interviewer received answers like: "Eskimo," "Puerto Rican," "Italian," "Hispanic," "Asian Indian," "Filipino," "half and half."

Eskimo? "Yes," explained the petite Chinese mother (Case 7). "My deceased husband was a huge Irishman. My children are dark complexioned. They have black hair and high cheekbones, but they are tall and husky like their father, not like Chinese who are small framed like me." On the other hand, a number of other parents proudly said their children were very good-looking. There was no way to confirm the parents' perception since this interviewer only met a few of the offspring.

A faculty member at Brown University, herself a partner in an intermarriage, commented on how looks affect the acceptance or rejection of an interracial child. She said:

> At Brown, I came across many children of mixed parentage. Most of them are gorgeous. The ones like that could be picked out, and they would say, 'I have no problems; I could go into this place or that. I have never encountered racism.' Then there are those who are funny looking. Like little Mr. Potato Heads. It's sad. It seems that they never fit into any group. Our society, which is so preoccupied with appearances, have really victimized these children where they have been so rejected based upon what they look like.

A confirmation of this statement was demonstrated at an Asian American Conference at the University of California in Berkeley, where four panelists presented findings from their research on the biracial experience. All four were of mixed Japanese ancestry. The female had long, straight, light brown hair, fair skin and sharp facial features. She grew up in the Midwest and had no discernible Asian looks. Her experiences as a biracial were totally positive. It was only when her family moved West that she became keenly interested in her Japanese heritage.

Another panelist resembled the popular image of Jesus. His wavy, dark-brown hair was worn shoulder length. His skin coloring was very-white without a trace of olive or tan. He wore a beard and he was tall and angular. Judging from appearance at first glance, one would say he was Lebanese. This man felt excluded, alienated, isolated, especially from Asian American groups that he tried to penetrate. He wanted desperately to join the Asian American movement, but the comments he received were, "So, you're interested in Asian Americans? Gee, I can't even tell you're Asian. I thought you were white!" "We were hoping that you'd look more Japanese (Murphy-Shigematsu, 1987).

The other two men had a combination of Japanese-Caucasian features; they were very handsome. It was obvious that physical appearance was a strong factor in how they were perceived and received, and they made this point in their presentations. There was a tendency for those who looked more Asian to be accepted within the Asian group and those who looked more white to be rejected. On the other hand, white features made them more acceptable to whites. When biracial students of mine were asked if they had ever encountered discrimination, those who were perceived as Caucasian said no; those who looked mixed or Asian said yes.

Siblings Who Look Different

Photos accompanying an article in Newsweek (1984:120) titled "Children of the Rainbow" show the shades and hues of offspring of mixed marriages. A daughter sitting next to her white father is dark black. Her brother on the lap of her dark mother is very light complexioned. In a mixed family, there is no assurance what color the siblings will be. In situations like these it must be difficult for siblings to relate to one another. Would they feel less like brother and sister? Would the parents favor the lighter skin over the darker skin ones? Would they favor the one who looked themselves. Within the black community, there is a hierarchy of social ranking based upon skin color. The lighter shades enjoy higher status.

Shame or Rejection of Parents

Children want to be proud of their parents. When one parent is a minority group member, the children, especially in their teenage years, may feel shame and want to hide that fact from public knowledge. One father (Case 29) told how his eldest son refused to walk or be seen with his parents in the street. He always ran far ahead of them. The father was quite aware that the boy did not want to be seen with his Chinese mother. Another interviewee, a black father (Case 4), remembered how his son would request to go ahead on the bus to wherever the family was going. Aware of his son's motives, the father would insist, "No, if we go, we go as a family."

Kich (1982) tells of another incident: "As a child, he tried to 'slip' his friend past his mother because 'I didn't want them to think my mother was strange, her speaking Japanese. . . . I didn't want them to talk to her. I look back on it and I think I must have really hurt her. . . . I felt ashamed, very ashamed of her because she was different."

A young college student revealed this parental rejection poignantly. In a paper she wrote:

> My (Chinese) father can't be held entirely responsible for the separation that developed between us when I was growing up. Part of the distancing was a conscious effort on my part. I went through a phase when I rejected him along with my Asian self. I was embarrassed by his imperfect English (yet he was a college professor), his unusual mannerisms and his non-Western looks. If I had a choice whether to be picked up in the car by my mother or him, I would automatically choose my mother. If a parent of mine needed to attend parents' night at school, I would pray that it would be my mother.
>
> . . . I used to fantasize what my life would be like if my mother had married another Caucasian and I came out 100 percent white.

Two other instances serve as illustrations of shame and rejection of parents during the teen years: One son angrily asked his mother, "Why did you have to marry a Chinaman?" Another boy never gave his mother the notes sent home by his teacher inviting her to school functions or parents' meetings. Curious to know why there was never any response to her notes, the teacher paid a visit to the boy's home and discovered that he was trying to hide the fact that his mother was Asian. Throughout Han Suyin's (1965) book *The Crippled Tree*, the author expressed how she despised being the daughter of a white woman in revolutionary China, where whites were blamed for China's ills. She went out of her way to be rebellious and difficult, knowing that it would incur her mother's wrath. She intentionally inflicted pain upon her mother because she was of the hated white race.

Cultural Factors and Ethnic Affiliation

Though intermarried partners may be quite accepting of each other's cultural traditions and customs, they tend to revert to their own childhood experiences for direction in rearing their own children. If for no other reason, they may have no other role models or they may have no precedent to follow when rearing children in a multiple cultural setting.

As previously mentioned, a Chinese intermarriage in the United States may involve more than two cultures. There is the dominant American culture, the Chinese culture and a third one reflecting the spouse's ethnic background. If both partners are strongly assimilated into the American way of life, there is fairly uniform consensus in attitudes, values, customs and behavior. Culturally speaking, the marriage is a homogenous one. Nevertheless, vestiges of ethnic heritage tend to persist, especially with the Chinese who are predominantly a first generation immigrant group. Jews and Catholics are particularly strong in their religious identities. Being black carries with it a heavy burden of minority status. When the marriage partners are strongly attached to or identified with their own ethnic beliefs and cultures, the parents may disagree on how the children should be brought up.

For example, a Chinese mother wants her son to excel academically, so she insists that his schoolwork comes first and refuses to let him join the Little League or basketball team. The Italian American father thinks the mother is making a sissy out of his son and wants him to participate in some rough and tumble sport. On a Saturday morning, if the mother says, "Stay home and study," and the father says, "Go play ball," the boy is baffled. If the Chinese mother wants her children to know her language and speaks to them only in Chinese, her Jewish husband may feel left out of conversations. On the other hand, he may insist that the children attend Hebrew school. These differences may degenerate into a power play between the husband and the wife. When what might have been a difference of opinion becomes a test of wills, trouble ensues. Even when the best of intentions are operating, and the parents think they can do a balancing act, realities may turn out quite differently from what they expected. Ponder the words of this expectant mother (Case 33):

> I will teach my children the language from the very beginning. When nursing, I will speak to my baby in Taiwanese. With Daddy he will speak Mandarin (her husband is Caucasian, but knows Mandarin). With Grandma, he will speak English. I do not anticipate any problems. When a child grows up with languages, he will absorb them.

This mother-to-be may be overly idealistic. In fact, she may find language inculcation in her child more difficult than she realizes, but she is on the right track in trying to expose her child to the rich cultural heritage from both parental backgrounds. If she is willing to put in the extra effort, her children will be enriched. However, teaching a child three tongues instead of one, will be more difficult.

Fumiko and Steve (Case 42) love to dress their little girl up for annual photos for the grandparents, first in kimono and obi for Fumiko's parents who are Japanese and then in Chinese jacket and trousers for Steve's parents who are Chinese. James (Case 35), who is divorced from his wife, makes a special effort to be with his daughter on Chinese New Year's. He goes to public school with her on that day and presents a special program for the class on celebrations and traditions of the holiday. When he explains that instead of gifts, children get little red envelopes with money in them, and he passes out red envelopes, all of his daughter's classmates wish they were Chinese.

As is evident, rearing the multiracial offspring involves extra effort to expose the children to both parental cultures, but children can also become the cause of rivalry between the parents if one or the other feels threatened by the diminution of one's own ethnic identity.

Parental Mistakes

When parents come from different religious backgrounds, and if they think that they should leave the choice of religion to the offspring, studies have shown that the child will grow up without any religion at all. So it is with other values and traditions which must be inculcated or there will be a void. George Kich (1982), in his study of biracial Japanese offspring, found that the parents of his subjects tended to avoid telling their children about their ethnic identity, thus creating a mystique that was detrimental to their personal development. Mistakenly, the parents may have refrained from mentioning, practicing or observing their ethnic traditions to avoid conflict with their mates. However, Kich found that "lack of communication about interracial marriage and identity issues, especially with fathers regardless of ethnicity, created a discontinuous and sometimes fragmented understanding of the family, its history, relatives and culture" (p. 209). Sometimes the offspring viewed this silence as a coverup of something undesirable. At some point in their lives, they will start a restless search for their roots, as was brought out in the following comments by a biracial offspring, son of a German father and a Japanese mother:

> As a child I was outwhiting the whites. It was an inferiority complex . . . . There was one event when I came to grips with my Asian American-ness. I had to write a paper and I wrote on the Japanese internment. I read 40 books on the subject. I couldn't stop. My grades plummeted in physics and other courses. I was sitting there crying. I talked to my Japanese grandmother and learned that side of myself. My mother never told me any of this.

The daughter of a Chinese Indonesian father and a Dutch mother, also told how she sought her Asian heritage after her marriage to a Chinese man:

> I learned about cultural differences from a Swiss guy that I had a relationship with, not from my parents. After that experience, I started reading eastern philosophy, doing Tai-Chi. I felt very attracted to eastern philosophy in idea and theory. I am not sure I was looking for roots. Curiosity at first. When opportunity presented itself for social experience, it was great. Maybe it was a search. I went to Asia for four weeks. I felt very socially secure . . . . Only now when I am 28 can I speak to my parents about my ideas of family upbringing. Now that I live with my Chinese mother-in-law I can understand my father better.

If there is one message to be garnered from the above two interviewees and George Kich's study of mixed Japanese offspring, it is that parents in an intermarriage must expose their children to their cultural heritages. To do less is to deprive these children of cultural nutrients essential to their psycholog-ical well-being. Children need to feel culturally rooted. If one culture is suppressed, the child may feel that half of him or her is inferior. If both cultures are left out, there will be a void.

GRANDPARENTS

Parental objection to intermarriage may be the biggest hurdle encountered by the couple, but when grandchildren arrive, the hostility and anger gen-erally dissipate and the little ones are accepted by the grandparents, of course with exceptions. In several instances, grandmothers take care of the children when the mothers work. With one couple (Case 27), the Hispanic grandmother looks after her granddaughter on weekdays, and the Chinese grand-mother babysits on weekends. It was the black grandmother (Case 46) who helped raise all seven of her grandchildren while the Chinese mother went out to work.

In several cases culled from the files of two Chinatown social service agencies, the grandmothers became surrogate mothers when their daughters abdicated their roles. In one case, the 30-year old Chinese mother had given birth to two children, a son age 11 and a daughter age 4. The father of the son is an Hispanic man from whom the mother is separated. The father of the daughter is a black man with whom she is presently involved. Grandma takes care of both children, and the boy calls his grandmother "Mother" since she is the main caretaker. He speaks mainly Chinese, but looks Hispanic. The girl looks black and has no visible Chinese features.

Grandma takes very good care of the children. She opposed her daughter's marriages, but accepted the grandchildren. The whole family, consisting of Grandma's three sons and their wives and children, live in a multiple family dwelling in Brooklyn. The social workers say the uncles never intentionally ostracized their sister's children, but because of their physical features, they really stick out in the family. The children are brought up in an entirely Chinese atmosphere among the brood of Chinese cousins. Lately, the boy has been acting out and his psychological and social behavior brought him to the attention of the school counselor. Grandma says she can no longer control the boy.

At another social service agency, there were two other similar cases. The first also involved a Chinese woman and a Hispanic young man. The woman's family cut her off until the baby arrived. Even though the grandparents were displeased, they took in the baby girl. The mother left the state, making her parents the legal guardians of her child. According to the social workers, the girl, now ten years old, is a very beautiful child. She is very smart, but hyperactive. The social workers say in cases like these, it is difficult to work with the grandparents because there is a two generation gap instead of one.

The other case involved a Chinese woman and an American Indian hus-band. They met in school and were married for five years. There is one child from the marriage. The maternal grandmother is taking care of both her daughter, who is emotionally ill, and the granddaughter. The grandmother is very supportive as is the rest of the family. They offered to send the child to a private boarding school. The social workers observed that even when Chinese families do not approve of their children's behavior, if a problem arises they will still rally to their sides. They consider it a family obligation.

In each of these instances, though the grandmothers provided a home and care for the grandchildren, they could not make up for the children's own awareness of their physical differences and the neglect or abandonment of the natural parents.

PERSONAL PERSPECTIVE OF BIRACIAL OFFSPRING

What Are You?

This question, "What are you?" evoked comments filled with anger, hostility and resentment to the utter surprise of this researcher. The following are a few representative responses:

> As a youngster in elementary school, people didn't know where to place me. I would pretend and play games. I would be the actor. Sometimes I pretended that I was Eskimo, sometimes Indian. I would make up stories. I never said I was Chinese or Dutch. I just said I was born in America. Then they wanted to know what nationality, and I would say, 'American.' If they were not appeased by that answer, then I would say, 'Eurasian.' If they still wanted to know further, then I would go into parental background.

Why was this person so hesitant about revealing that she was of Chinese-Dutch heritage? Was Eskimo or Indian more intriguing than Chinese-Dutch? She said she always felt uncomfortable when people questioned her background and she sensed that others were equally unsure of how to react when they could not neatly place her within one racial category.

A young man with multiple racial makeup—Chinese, German, Portugese and Hawaiian—said:

> People here, when they look at me, are hesitant as to what to say or how to act because my racial makeup gets in the way of a more personal relationship. That seems to be the factor that they put into the equation as to whether they want to know me, or how to treat me.

A young man whose father was black and mother white gave this reply:

> What am I? I dread responding to that question. Sometimes I say I am black; sometimes I say I am white. Most of the time I say black.

When does this young man say black? When he is with a black group? When does he say white? When he is with a white group? Does he switch to feel that he is part of the group he is with at the moment? Is it necessary to label oneself exclusively white or black when one can claim membership in both? Why were they not taught to be proud of being mixed?

A young lady of Chinese white parentage wrote:

> Sometimes I feel guilty that I can't balance my dual racial identity. I would like to be equally secure, equally proud of my two racial components, but it doesn't happen that way. When I introduced myself to people as a child and junior high school student, I would say, "I'm only

half Chinese," deemphasizing my Asian identity and bringing out my Caucasian ancestry which was not always apparent to the observer. Sometimes I still introduce myself as being "only half-Chinese." Now, however, I do so in an apologetic manner expressing that I'm sorry I can't be full-blooded, genuine Chinese. The shame has shifted from the Chinese identity to the Caucasian identity . . . .

People often ask me, "How do you define yourself? The answer to that question is simply that I don't. I don't define myself as anything; I simply let others try to define me.

A young lady of German-Filipino parentage noted that:

When people ask you that question, they don't stop with that line of questioning. When you say you are German-Filipino, they might say, 'You don't look it.' I always feel that I have to defend myself. I am offended by the question. Sometimes it isn't even a question. People across the room would be trying to figure out what you are, and they would point a finger at you, and you knew what they were trying to do. The gesture alone carried negative connotations.

How does one interpret this response from one interviewee? "My father is Japanese and my mother isn't." The answer confirms the hesitancy of mixed offspring to give a forthright answer. The same sort of answer came from another person of Japanese-black parents:

When a black leader asked me that question, I said I was black and something else. He interpreted that to mean that I wanted to disassociate myself from the black power movement. He wanted me to say I was black. He wants to know whose side you are on. It's a personal decision that is very stressful.

This researcher did not anticipate this type of response to a presumably innocuous question put to a group of mixed offspring at a roundtable discussion at a Cornell University seminar. Obviously, the question "What are you?" touched off sensitive nerves frayed by incessant curiosity against people who did not fit into neat categories.

. . . the uncategorized biracial person is an outsider to every group. This marginal position has meant confusion, rejection and alienation. . . . Not only is the biracial person's ethnic and racial heritage confused and contested by each group, but the biracial person's loyalty to the politics and aspirations of each group is questioned as well (Kich, 1982:3).

To further confirm the confusion in the minds of biracials about their identities, Gunde (1971) asked 29 Japanese white respondents, "What do you put down on forms requiring racial or ethnic identification?" Eleven said "other," an innocuous nonidentity. Seven said "Japanese American" or "Oriental." Two said "white." Six said, "part-Japanese or part-white," and three said, "we leave it blank."

"Passing into the safe and assured categorization of one race or the other has been one option for those biracial people whose appearance and language ability did not mark them as different" (Kich, 1982:31). However, passing is accompanied with guilt of self-denial and fear of detection.

> . . . the more she passed, the more anxious and frightened of exposure she became. 'I was covering up. . . . I didn't bring people home' (Kich, 1982:108).

Given the unequal social and economic valuations ascribed to race in this country, the biracial person usually seeks to be included in the majority or superior group, but generally is not accepted by that group. In Hall's study of black Japanese persons (Kich, 1982, *See*, also, Murphy-Shigematsu, 1987), 60 percent chose to identify with blacks apparently because other blacks most easily accepted them.

Asian white biracials find it easier to associate with other Asians. Mixed Chinese offspring feel more comfortable in a Chinese setting. When asked about his ethnic identity, Tony, who is one-fourth Chinese, said, "I'm American." Yet, he is president of a local chapter of a well-known Chinese American organization. He is married to a woman who is 7/8 Chinese, and he is deeply involved in Chinese American issues. Why? "Because I feel very comfortable among Chinese."

Victor related his experiences as a person of mixed Chinese blood. He is in his early twenties.

> My father is German Jewish and my mother is Chinese. I was brought up on a college campus. My father is a professor of Chinese history. My mother came from a very prominent family in China. She taught Chinese literature. My father speaks Mandarin and I was brought up with constant exposure to Chinese culture, but I consciously shunned or avoided learning the language or culture. I only started to learn Chinese within the last three or four years, but I am fluent in Mandarin now. In my last year's class in Chinese in college, I covered three years work in one.
>
> It started when my father asked if I wanted to join a delegation to China. That trip made a great difference in my life. It was tough the first time. I didn't know the language. Afterwards, all things started to happen. I changed physically. I started to look different. I had the best year academically. I started to discover what I could do as a part-Chinese. I liked the new feeling. I started learning the language and started exploring all the possibilities. I've made five more trips to China since.

Victor went through a total transformation after he came back from his trip to China. For the first 20 years of his life, he tried to distance himself from that part of him that was Chinese. How does he explain the change? "It has to do with my going there. I saw the people, their way of life. I saw my family, and I saw conditions and history, and my family was part of it. My Chinese family accepted me as part of the family without hesitation.

The experiences of a biracial child was strong enough to lead George Kich (1982) to write his doctoral dissertation on the subject of "Ethnic/Racial Identity Development in Biracial Japanese-White Adults." Whereas no known research has been conducted on mixed offspring from Chinese intermarriages, a number of studies have been done on biracial Japanese. Reasons for this are that the Japanese are more of a native born population and the Chinese in the United States are still very much an immigrant population. As noted in Chapter 2, the rate of Japanese intermarriage is higher. Also, a considerable number of Japanese women married American soldiers following the occupation of Japan after World War II, resulting in a large number of Japanese biracial offspring. In the absence of research on Chinese biracials, some inference can be drawn from the Japanese experience.

Three Stage Progression

In his dissertation, Kich delineated three stages that the biracial Japanese white person goes through. The first stage is the painful feeling of being different and separate from others, stemming from lack of communication about race in the family.

> . . . Respondent No. 3 said, "You look in the mirror; 'who the fuck am I?' I don't look like anybody!" His painful experience of not belonging included rejection from the Japanese American Nisei cohort with whom he felt the most affinity, a sense of profound difference ("displaced") from white Americans, and an appearance that was unlike anyone else he knew (p. 73).

The second stage for the Japanese white biracial is characterized by self-labeling and an active search and pursuit of his or her heritage by learning the language, contacting relatives and reading about and traveling to Japan. Most of Kich's subjects wanted to know more about their Japanese roots. This type of behavior was also noted in the Chinese biracials. As Siu Sin Far (1987) wrote:

> Whenever I have the opportunity, I steal away to the library and read every book I can find on China and the Chinese. I learn that China is the oldest civilized nation on the face of the earth and a few other things. At eighteen years of age what troubles me is not that I am what I am, but that others are ignorant of my superiority (p. 174).

By the third stage, the biracial Japanese white accepts his or her dual heritage, but also recognizes the need for an interracial reference group. For Japanese biracials, this condition is more easily met because there are more of them. An interracial reference group for offspring of mixed Chinese parentage may be something that is farther into the future.

When one thinks of biracial children, one tends to think of dualities. However, children of Chinese intermarriages may be combinations of many ethnic or racial groups. One mate is Chinese, but the other may be Gentile white, Jewish white, the range of Hispanic and Asian groups, American black, Caribbean black, or American Indian. All these groups were represented, even in our small sample of cases, so that a Chinese Jewish offspring's experience will not be the same as that of a Chinese Japanese or Chinese black child. Variations are so great that a biracial reference group may be somewhat meaningless.

How will this biracial reference group be labeled? What do they want to call themselves? As was pointed out above, there is a great deal of confusion even in self-identification. Kich says his respondents' preference was for "Eurasian." This term was used for offspring of Europeans who went to Asia and married Asian spouses there. It cannot apply to Asians who marry blacks, Hispanics and Asians of varying ethnic groups in this country. Another term is "Amerasian," a combination of American and Asian. The term carries a much larger identity and is much more inclusive. However, the term has been applied more recently to offspring of American soldiers stationed in Asia and local women there. Children of intermarriages in this country may have to fall back upon the term "biracial."

Dealing with the Duality

In spite of the fact that our society wants to categorize people racially or ethnically, parents of interracial children must counter this attempt by teaching their children that they are and can be members of both races. Says Dr. P.H. Baptiste, Jr. (1983), professor of multicultural education at the University of Houston:

> Parents must utilize their uniqueness as a positive environmental factor. As members of two different races, each must provide the child with a positive model of the respective race and access to their respective race's cultural customs and practices. The child can be made to realize that his or her uniqueness is a precious and beautiful bond between Mother and Father.
>
> . . . Interracial children are usually stared at or treated as an oddity when in public gatherings. This can be damaging to a child if parents tend to

ignore this 'people' characteristic. Discuss this incident when it happens to you and your child. Be sure that your child understands that there is nothing wrong with him or her.

The fundamental problem in the duality is that minority groups are assigned lower social status according to color and ethnicity. When the mixed child aspires to membership in the higher status group, he is rebuffed. And his attempts to gain entry is often accompanied by guilt for denial of the other part of him. The tendency is to disassociate himself from a group encumbered with inferior status and unfavorable stereotypes, so he searches hard for positive attributes of that culture to reaffirm himself. He is comforted in that knowledge, but his lament is that others do not see him as he sees himself. That was Siu Sin Far's dilemma. With higher social status now accorded Chinese and Japanese in this country, the duality may be less of a problem when they marry white, but the problem will persist if the union is with black, Hispanic or native American.

This may be why Cynthia Nakashima (1987), herself a *Nikkei hapa* (half Japanese), refutes the totally negative aspects of being biracial. In her study of Californian and Hawaiian Japanese biracial subjects, she found that they have a clear sense of self, a confidence in negotiating both Japanese and white communities, and a keen interest in Japanese culture and community. Using an ethnic identity questionnaire, she shows Nikkei hapa to be especially high—indeed even higher than first generation Japanese in several cases—in attachment to Japanese values, language and organizations. In fact, she believes that mixed Japanese have arrived at a successful integration of core values with "white" values as filtered through a third vantage point, that of one who is neither Japanese nor white.

Dr. Man Keung Ho (1984), an intermarriage counselor and professor of social work at the University of Oklahoma, also sees the positive side for mixed offspring:

> Through exposure to both parents' religious and ethnic cultures, children from a successful intermarriage tend to have a greater opportunity to learn and to express themselves. They are likely to have a heightened awareness, a harmonious integration of themselves and their environment, a satisfying relationship with themselves, and enriched relationships with others.

Dr. Ho's outlook lends credence to the contention that interracial offspring tend to be more innovative, more creative because they see things from more than one perspective, they experience differences, and therefore they can appreciate and build upon a broader cultural base.

M. Seeman agrees and "argues that an ambiguous social position need not necessarily cause psychological distress—on the contrary, it may be a positive experience for the marginal individual. He reminds us that both Park and Stonequist noted the potential for creativity, innovation and leadership among occupants of marginal positions." (A. Wilson, 1984:48–49).

Ann Wilson asks: Can children of interracial marriages escape marginality only by gravitating toward one or the other group? Is it possible for these offspring to steer a successful course between groups? Yes, she concludes. Individuals in modern day are more flexible. They must juggle their identities to fit the situation. One may be Chinese in one setting, American in another, Jewish, Hispanic or black in other settings according to the social situation or environment in which one finds oneself. This is termed "situational ethnicity" (p.50). For example, the two girls in the Chinese Jewish family are Jewish when they go to the synagogue. They are Chinese when they attend Chinese school. They are American when they march as Girl Scouts in the Memorial Day parade. They are enriched by many cultural streams. But even if the offspring of mixed parentage can subjectively resolve the question of their duality to their own satisfaction, can they resolve it objectively by getting others to accept them in their situational ethnic roles?

Having presented the findings from research studies and from interviews with biracials, it can be stated that, at this point in time, children of a mixed union do have a more complicated set of variables to sort through and parents do face an added dimension to their child-rearing responsibilities.

9

Dynamics of Change

There is no turning back to the days when intermarriage was deterred by physical isolation of groups, by strong social sanctions, by legal proscription and by negative attributes. Some of these forces continue to operate, but they are losing ground. The incidence of outmarriage is increasing and opposition to it is lessening, but what we know of mixed unions is sparse, mythical, erroneous or conjectural. Since intermarriage is a social phenomenon of the future, it behooves us to learn as much about it as we can.

The increasing incidence of intermarriage is a recent social happening. Endogamy or inmarriage has been the standard for centuries. This departure from the standard requires a new perspective and new rules. These have not been developed, so people still look at intermarriage as a deviance and abberation. When they feel uncomfortable, they react unfavorably.

CHANGES IN FAMILIES

Marriage creates a new family unit, but characteristics of the family have also undergone tremendous transformation. Marriage used to be a family affair where parental say was absolute or dominant. Parents secured mates for their offspring and the predominant concerns were continuity of the family name, perpetuation of the group, procreation of children and establishment of a social and economic unit.

In modern urban society, these functions of the family are no longer predominant. The uppermost concern in a marriage today is complementary spousal fulfillment. Carrying on the family name and group preservation are inconsequential considerations when two people decide to marry. The small size of households nowadays already attests to the reduced importance of procreation of children in family values. In most instances, the family no longer functions as a productive economic unit. Husband and wife go off to their respective jobs and are only together in the evenings or weekends. Familial functions, instead of being multipurpose, are now concentrated on personal spousal relations. This two person relationship is intimate, intense and exclusive. There must be strong, mutual physical and emotional attachments between them, and the relationship is symbiotic. Husband and wife must satisfy almost all of each other's emotional needs. This is the way today's marital relations have been redefined.

If the functions of a marriage have been redefined, the basis for selection of a marital partner has also undergone change. The spouse will select a mate more in line with the ability of the other to satisfy his or her personal needs, and selection will be based not so much on racial or ethnic considerations, but on personal attributes of the individual. In a larger sense, this is a decided shift to Western values of individualism. A marriage partner is selected for his or her attractiveness and personality at the height of romantic passion. However, an individual cannot shed one's cultural heritage completely, and as life settles down to a more mundane pattern in marriage, differences in background, beliefs and ethnicity creep into the picture. The resolution of these differences is the added dimension to tensions in an intermarriage.

GREATER STRESS AND STRAIN

As an intermarriage counselor and himself party to an outmarriage, Dr. Man Keung Ho (1984) minced no words when he wrote in his book, *Building a Successful Intermarriage*: "Intermarriage has been treated in the past as an abnormality, defiance or disgrace.... When persons of different ethnic, racial or religious background marry, their adjustment difficulties are likely to greatly exceed those of couples of the same background. To the normal differences in personality, social class, education and life experiences must be added the differences in values, customs and traditions associated with different ethnicities, races and religions" (pp. 28 and 49). Dr. Ho starts out with the premise that an intermarriage is more difficult than an endogamous one and will require more effort to make it successful. This study arrived at the same conclusion.

This chapter summarizes the findings, tries to answer some of the most commonly asked questions and takes a look at the future. If there is no turning back the tide of intermarriage, then what will the tide bring with it? Invariably, the first question that comes to the fore is: What is the extent of intermarriage?

IS INTERMARRIAGE ON THE RISE?

From examination of marriage license applications in the five boroughs of New York City for two years, 1972 and 1982, it was found that rates of outmarriage remained level at 15 percent of the number of Chinese applicants and at 27 percent for both years when recalculated on the basis of number of marriages. Surprisingly, the rates have not risen to any extent since Schwartz' (1951) study covering the period 1931 to 1938. At that time, the outmarriage rate for Chinese in New York City was 26 percent. These are the only two studies ever conducted on Chinese intermarriage in New York City. Although the rates remained level over these forty odd years, the absolute number of mixed marriages has increased, but not to the extent originally surmised. When compared to rates of 41 percent in Los Angeles and 76 percent in Hawaii based on marriages as noted by Kitano in 1979, the New York City rates are low.

Basically, reasons for these low rates are three: New York City's Chinese population has increased phenomenally, and population size has definite negative correlation with the rate of outmarriage. A larger Chinese population means that there are more choices within one's own ethnic group. It also means stronger community cohesion and social sanction. A second, equally impacting factor is a more balanced sex ratio, and the third factor is that New York City's Chinese population is more than three-fourths foreign born or first generation. Immigrants come to this country already imbued with a strong sense of national identity and cultural traits. They are very different from the native born, who are acculturated to the American way of thinking. Generation has been shown to be a decisive factor in intermarriage. This was clearly demonstrated in Leonetti and Newell-Morris' (1982) chart pertaining to the Japanese in Seattle. Outmarriage among the first generation was practically nil. By the second generation, the rate had risen to the 20 percent level. By the third generation, the rate had soared to as high as 50 percent.

ARE INTERMARRIAGES LESS STABLE?

A commonly held assumption is that intermarriages tend to end up in divorce. That is the greatest concern and fear for all involved. Past studies on Chinese intermarriages, primarily in Hawaii but also in Los Angeles, Iowa and Kansas, all answer in the affirmative (*See*, Table 17). Yes, the divorce rate is much higher with the outmarried than the inmarried. The latest study was done in Hawaii by Schewertfeger (1982) and covered the period from 1968 to 1976. Amazingly during this period of time, there were no divorces at all for the inmarried couples, whereas the divorce rate for Chinese males outmarrying was 18.7 per 100 marriages and for Chinese females, was 14.1. The findings were consistent. Divorce rates were considerably higher for Chinese who married outside of their own ethnic group, and these marriages were much more fragile when the groom was Chinese.

In another study, Michael Miller (1971) looked at the duration of marriages of divorces granted couples in Hawaii for two periods, 1952 to 1954 and from 1962 to 1964. Most studies of intermarriage have utilized Hawaiian figures because that is where large scale intermarriage has taken place, the social climate is more accepting of mixed unions and the statistics are readily available. Even under these optimum conditions, the mean duration of marriages before breakup is shorter for outmarriages than inmarriages. For the 1952 to 1954 period, inmarriages ending in divorce lasted 9.5 years, whereas outmarriages for Chinese males who eventually divorced lasted only 7.23 years and for Chinese females 6.29 years. In the second period, 1962 to 1964, the duration of marriages for the inmarried before divorce was 13.11 years. For the outmarried Chinese male it was 9.29 and for the Chinese female it was 7.42 years. Thus, according to other researchers, intermarriage was less stable, breakup was more likely and the marriages did not last as long.

This study develops a slightly different picture. Using our 50 case studies, six of the marriages had already broken up and three were a bit shaky. That results in a 12 to 18 percent rate. When compared to the divorce rate of the general population in New York City of 40 percent for the year 1982 (69,100 marriages divided by 27,756 divorces), the Chinese outmarriage divorce rate is comparatively low. A more accurate picture would be derived by comparing Chinese inmarried divorce rates to outmarried rates. This was done in Chapter Five using divorce figures compiled by the New York State Department of Health. By comparing the number of inmarriage divorces over inmarriages and the number of outmarriage divorces over outmarriages, it was found that breakups were proportionately about the same for both in and outmarriages. It seems that the intermarital pattern for Chinese in New York City does not conform to that for other parts of the country. However, these data are scanty and more research is warranted.

DO INTERMARRIAGES ENCOUNTER MORE OBSTACLES?

Just as mixed marriages are presumed to be unstable, they are also presumed to encounter more obstacles. This study examined the areas that could cause trouble. The most glaring of these are family objections. The painful choice had to be made between acceding to parental wishes and giving up one's intended, or defying one's parents and marrying out. There is no way of knowing how many took the first choice and backed out. Our case studies dealt with those who persevered, but family disapproval was manifest and strong. In many instances, it delayed the marriage for years. Parental disappointment was keen, and in some cases parental ties were severed.

In his counseling practice, both in therapy sessions and in interviews, Dr. Man Keung Ho (1984) found that rejection by parents, especially in the early part of the marriage, constitutes one of the most destructive obstacles to successful intermarriage. Imagine how great the sense of nonacceptance must be for Bryant (Case 32) whose father-in-law insists upon referring to him as Vivian's friend rather than her husband, even after six years of marriage. Sylvia's (Case 13) father won't even recognize that she is married. And Grace's (Case 30) mother won't utter her son-in-law's name, referring to him as "that man" or "him." These rejection tactics can put a great strain upon the marriage.

Since most of the outmarrying couples interviewed were highly educated, more mature in age, more assimilated into Western culture and more cosmopolitan in outlook, they were better able to cope with the differences in their personal, physical and cultural backgrounds. Being in New York had its advantages. The diversity, the anonymity, the higher degree of tolerance and the fact that both spouses generally work operated to reduce the exclusiveness of the marital relationship. The couples were in surprising agreement on most values. Their disagreements were more along the lines of personal habits or personality traits and such disagreements are typical of all marriages. Therefore, it can be stated that higher socioeconomic background is a factor in better intermarital adjustment. It seems that lower class couples experienced more difficulty as exemplified in the cases taken from Chinese social service agencies.

In many instances, the non-Chinese spouse had a strong leaning toward the Chinese in the first place and the Chinese spouse was already strongly imbued with Western values. In fact, five out of the fifty couples in this study were married in China or Taiwan. In many cases, both parties were completely assimilated to the American way of life and there were few cultural differences between them. This was especially true for the second generation Chinese who had had little contact with other Chinese. Religion posed no problem for the intermarrying couples. The Chinese partner was quite willing to accept the religious practices of the mate because of a more tolerant religious heritage.

The one notable behavioral pattern observed was the tendency of the couples not to attend Chinese functions together. On many occasions, the non-Chinese spouse did not attend because he or she could not understand what was going on, felt out of place or simply did not enjoy going. Yet many intermarried Chinese were community activists and attended many meetings and festivities. The absence of the spouse on such occasions was conspicuous.

Most interviewees could not come up with many examples of cultural conflicts or with only superficial ones. Basically, the couples must have had a lot in common and felt comfortable with one another, otherwise they would not have made the important decision to marry. If both partners had been brought up in the United States and educated in American schools, their backgrounds would have been similar. In fact, they would be more at ease in an American setting than a Chinese one. Similarity in class background was also a factor. High educational attainment was evident with the intermarrying couples. Using the much larger population base of census data from 1980, 55 percent of the Chinese men and 72 percent of the Chinese women who married out had a college education. Over nine out of ten of our interviewees had some college education. That meant a greater tolerance for differences and a greater appreciation for diversity.

Marrying later in life meant that the couples were more mature, and outmarrying couples were older at the time of marriage. For some, the courtship period was rather lengthy and gave them plenty of time to find out whether they were right for each other. Noted also was the artistic or unconventional bent of the outmarried. They were willing to buck tradition and to risk any disapprobation that might follow. These were flexible, hearty souls, more adventuresome, more daring and most likely better able to withstand the greater vicissitudes of an intermarriage.

IS SOCIETY MORE ACCEPTING OF INTERMARRIAGES NOW?

When people do a double-take, turn around and stare at an interracial couple, they are not completely accepting, but if the worst they do is stare, then the degree of acceptance has come a long way. A Gallup poll on attitude toward intermarriage in 1968 revealed that only 20 percent approved and 72 percent disapproved. The other 8 percent were uncertain. Another poll was taken in 1978. At this time, 36 percent approved, 54 percent disapproved and 10 percent were uncertain. By 1983, 43 percent approved, 50 percent disapproved and 7 percent were uncertain (Collins, 1984). From these figures, one can surmise that intermarriage is gaining acceptance, although disapproval still exceeds approval.

Attending classes together, rubbing shoulders in public places, working along side one another, even living in the same neighborhood no longer evoke the intense opposition that they once did, and racial mixing has become commonplace. According to the assimilation theory of Milton Gordon, the next hurdle to scale after structural assimilation is the marital one. If you can answer "Yes," or "It doesn't matter," to the question "would you want your daughter to marry one?" that would be the ultimate acceptance. Marriage as the ultimate measure would mean the reduction of social distance between the ethnic groups and the lessening of racial prejudice. At one time, Chinese were second only to blacks as least desirable marriage partners. Now a more favorable image prevails.

Some Chinese have the notion that marrying white is marrying up. However, they may be in for a rude awakening when they find they are not totally accepted by whites, yet are looked down upon by the Chinese. More often than not, these Chinese are accepted in the larger society not because they married white, but because their professions or their achievements give them recognition or prestige. Within Chinese society, however, marrying out in most instances means a lowering of status, especially if the spouse is black, Hispanic or Japanese. The latter is a holdover from the historical enmity between China and Japan.

AN INDICATOR OF ASSIMILATION?

Is intermarriage an indicator of assimilation? Assimilate to what? It used to be toward the White Anglo Saxon Protestant model, but since the 1960s people are more accepting of cultural diversity. Pizzas and chow mein are just as American as hot dogs and apple pie. European immigrants once tried to shed their mother tongues and learn English as quickly as possible. Now it is *tres chic* to be able to speak a foreign language. In New York City especially, American culture is a conglomeration of many ethnic cultures. Walk down many New York streets and you will find a Greek restaurant next to an Indian restaurant next to a Chinese restaurant next to Kentucky Fried Chicken next to a McDonald's. Wearing a *yamulka* attracts no more attention than wearing a *sari*. In New York City, one can almost be as individualistic as one wishes in his or her lifestyle. There is no set American standard. This diversity creates an acceptance of differences perhaps not found in most places throughout the United States and provides a more receptive environment for persons in mixed marriages.

However, assimilation does mean embracing the American concepts and values of individualism, competitiveness, democracy, aggressiveness, innovation, freedom, openness, pleasure-seeking and the good life in terms of material possessions. It means shedding some of the Chinese values of family obligation, hard work, parental obedience, respect for elders, frugality and Chinese nationalism. Assimilation means using English as the dominant language of communication. It means adopting the mannerisms and customs of this country. It does not mean one must discard the use of the Chinese language or not observe the Chinese customs or traditions on occasions. It means they will be diluted. The above examples are not exhaustive but illustrative. However, one condition for assimilation is that the ethnic group must be accepted as American and the ethnic member must feel that he or she belongs.

In an intermarriage, since family objection continues to be so strong, the ethnic gap may be widened or exacerbated. Both parties will experience the rejection of the spouse's family and relatives based primarily on ethnicity. Yet, in their daily lives together after the marriage, each side will have to make compromises and come together. Since the Chinese ways will have less reinforcement, the strength of Chinese culture will diminish in favor of the prevailing American ways.

The cosmopolitan atmosphere of New York City has been repeatedly stressed as a favorable backdrop for mixed marriages, but this factor is counterbalanced by the strong and viable Chinese community that exerts considerable social control. The further one is removed from the Chinese community, whether that community is Chinatown or a circle of Chinese family, friends and relatives, the more likelihood of marriage outside of the Chinese fold.

In the long run, intermarriage speeds up acceptance of American ways—or it could be that, acceptance of American ways speeds up intermarriage. Will the speed-up result in further lowering of racial barriers like the desegregation of schools, the mixing of neighborhoods or integration of the workplace? It should, and it is another step along the path of integration.

FUTURE GENERATIONS

Biracial children of mixed Chinese parentage in the United States are few and far between. As stated previously, the Chinese population in the United States is very much a first generation one; earlier immigrants did not spawn a native born generation because they did not bring their women here. Nor did many Chinese females marry American soldiers like the Japanese, Korean, Filipinos and Vietnamese did. Literature dealing specifically with offspring of mixed Chinese unions is equally scarce. In many instances for this study, writings by Japanese biracials were alluded to because their situation is closest to that of the Chinese. Yet, it is not the same. A few Chinese biracials were interviewed, and their comments, experiences and feelings were noted in Chapter Eight.

A larger question posed by interracial marriages is whether the progeny of these mixed unions will create such a diverse group that physical and cultural features will be blurred enough to erase racial and national lines. The United States is a nation of immigrants. The earlier stock of European immigrants has created a dominant white American identity by admixture, now divided more along religious lines than physical characteristics. Presently, half of legal immigrants entering the country are Asians. To what extent will they be absorbed into the American population through outbreeding? For Chinese, at the moment, the absorption looks like a long way down the road. The outmarriage rate is not high, and those who outmarry tend to be better educated. Both variables of education and outmarriage are correlated with fewer offspring.

INFERIOR OR SUPERIOR BREED?

Another emotionally charged question regarding intermarriage is whether the genes of mixed race children combine to produce either an "inferior" or "superior" breed. In the past, the inferior premise predominated and was evident in such disparaging terms applied as mongrelization and miscegenation to mixed offspring. Even human geneticists lent credence to the theory of the dangers of racial crossing between widely separated races, as, for example, this quote by Professor East in *Genetic Principles in Medicine and Social Science* (Hogben, 1932) in the 1930s:

> The operation of the hereditary mechanism holds out only a negligible prospect of good results against the higher probability of bad results through disturbing the balance whole of each component ... When two varieties or races are crossed, 'succeeding generations will tend to combine all the hereditary units by which the original parents differed in every possible recombination.'"

Therefore, concluded human geneticist Professor East, miscegenation was "necessarily bad." However, he was chastised by his fellow scientists for "discussing this problem with a tacit acknowledgment of his own racial superiority."

Most human geneticists today hedge their comments about cross breeding between races. They will say increased vigor or heterosis has been amply demonstrated in plant cross breeding. "Hybrids will immediately display full vigor and are usually very much superior to both parents .... Increase in vigor after intercrossing between inbred lines has also been observed in animals; and there is every reason to assume that 'isolate breakage' in man, *i.e.*, marriages between individuals belonging to different isolates, will have a similar effect" (Muntzing, 1961). However, "genes for vigor as well as for various defects are certainly located in the same chromosomes and are, therefore, often linked. The linkage between genes, which act in a plus and minus direction, renders the production of extreme plus combinations very difficult" (Muntzing, 1961:272).

One of the most exacting studies on the Genetics of Interracial Crosses in Hawaii was done by Morton Newton, Chin S. Chung and Ming-Pi Mi (1967) during the period of 1958 to 1966. The purpose of their research was to answer two questions: 1) what are the genetic effects of outcrossing in man on the first generation hybrids and 2) do human populations represent coadapted genetic combinations that are disrupted after the first generation of outcrossing. In other words, what happens in subsequent generations when the children and grandchildren of mixed races have their families?

Scientific experiments performed on the fruit fly have shown that "viability was increased by heterozygosity and decreased by recombination." This means that the first generation offspring show increased vigor, but that subsequent generations may be less vigorous than the parental genotype. The reason advanced was "outbreeding produces novel genotypes, not yet subject to the sieve of natural selection" (Newton Morton, Chin S. Chung and Ming-Pi Mi, 1967:1).

For Morton, Chung and Mi, the social laboratory was Hawaii, chosen for its long history of racial admixture and its accessibility to racial statistics. The study was based upon 172,448 birth records and 6,879 fetal death certificates. Newborns and fetal deaths were used to delineate the physical from environmental factors. The premise was that heterosis in man is shown by changes in fertility and increased resistance to disease. The findings were:

1) That first and later generation hybrids in man suffer no appreciable loss of fertility, and may have indeed increased fertility, compared with the parental races (p. 57).

2) There is no significant hybridity effect on fetal or infant mortality (p. 85).

3) There is no critical evidence of any effect of hybridity or recombination on the frequency of congenital malformation. (p. 125).

The scientists concluded that "First generation hybrids between races in man are intermediate in size, mortality and morbidity between the parental groups, and at the present time, human populations do not represent coadapted genetic combinations which are disrupted by outcrossing" (p. 148). In other words, there is no scientific evidence to prove that there is regression in physical characteristics in subsequent generations from progeny in mixed marriages.

Scientific jargon aside, perhaps it is personal illusion or delusion on the part of this observer, offspring from mixed Chinese marriages seem to be unusually attractive, talented, creative and intelligent. Many are in the literary or performing arts. They seem to break out of the ethnic mold and enter fields seldom ventured by full-blooded Chinese Americans. A few biracials have distinguished themselves in spite of special problems and discrimination.

Han Suyin, Siu Sin Far (Edith Eaton) and Diana Chang were writers. Ruth Ann Koesun was a soloist and principal dancer with the American Ballet Theater for 23 years. Nancy Kwan is a well-known movie actress. Ron Darling is the New York Mets star pitcher. Dr. Franklin Chang-Diaz, astronaut, flew the Colombia space flight and returned to Earth safely. Claudia Liem was crowned Miss New York Teen in 1986 and was first runner-up in the national pageant. Mai Shan Ley was Miss U.S.A. of 1984. One of my students of Chinese-black parentage is a fashion model for an agency employing a large percentage of models of mixed parentage. The heterosis or increased vigor seems to be manifest in creativity, in beauty, in performance and in endowment in these mixed offspring.

Statistics from the marriage license applications show that one-third of the brides and grooms who are half Chinese marry Chinese, one-third marry whites or blacks and close to a third marry Hispanics. Generations branching off from these admixtures will not be biracial Chinese-Caucasian, but of many races and colors. What happens when the blood of many peoples and many nations course through our veins? Will we then be free of racism? The prospect of such a millenium is certainly a titillating one.

Appendix

FICTITIOUS NAMES AND CASE NUMBERS OF INTERVIEWEES
IF CITED IN CASE STUDIES

CASE NO.	HUSBAND*	ETHNICITY**	WIFE*	ETHNICITY**
1	John	WASP	Becky	Chinese
2	Melvin	Jewish	Sue May	Chinese
3	—	Chinese	—	White
4	George	Black	Elizabeth	Chinese
5	Warren	Chinese	Myra	Scot/Mixed
6	—	Chinese	—	Japanese
7	—	Irish	—	Chinese
8	—	Chinese	—	White
9	Irving	Jewish	Melody	Chinese
10	—	White	Mary	Chinese
11	Jason	Chinese	Carmen	Puerto Rican
12	Denis	Chinese	—	Yugoslavian
13	—	WASP	Sylvia	Chinese
14	—	Chinese	—	WASP
15	William	Chinese	Jean	WASP
16	—	WASP	Lily	Chinese
17	—	Chinese	—	Italian
18	—	White	—	Chinese
19	—	White	—	Chinese
20	Seth	Jewish	Flora	Chinese
21	Calvert	Italian	Yi-Fong	Chinese
22	Simon	Germ./ Catholic	Charlene	Chinese

FICTITIOUS NAMES AND CASE NUMBERS OF INTERVIEWEES
IF CITED IN CASE STUDIES (Continued)

CASE NO.	HUSBAND*	ETHNICITY**	WIFE*	ETHNICITY**
23	Peter	Lebanese	Carol	Chinese
24	—	Chinese	—	Irish
25	—	Chinese	—	Italian
26	Jack	Irish	Lucie	Chinese
27	Pierre	Puerto Rican	Esther	Chinese
28	—	E. Ind./Blk.	—	Chinese
29	Sam	WASP	Kun-yi	Chinese
30	—	Jewish	Grace	Chinese
31	—	Spanish	Wei Min	Chinese
32	Bryant	WASP	Vivian	Chinese
33	Frank	Germ./Irish	Chung-Li	Chinese
34	Nelson	Japanese	Helen	Chinese
35	James	Chinese	Sharon	Jewish
36	Noel	Black	Thelma	Chinese
37	Carlos	Chinese	—	Brazilian
38	Kenneth	Chinese	Sonia	Swedish
39	Paul	WASP	Debra	Chinese
40	Chi Yuan	Chinese	Ann	WASP
41	—	Chinese	—	WASP
42	Steve	Chinese	Fumiko	Japanese
43	Jospeh	Chinese	Linda	Jewish
44	Liang	Chinese	Julia	Germ./Amer.
45	Henry	Jewish	Chu-Lin	Chinese
46	Tom	Black	Jade	Chinese
47	Gordon	Germ./Irish	Mei-Hwa	Chinese
48	—	Chinese	—	German
49	—	Italian/Jew.	—	Chinese
50	—	Jewish	—	Chinese

Notes:　*　No name appears for those not specifically cited.

　　　　**　Ethnicity based upon self or spouse identity.

Bibliography

Adams, Romanzo
1937 "Chinese Familialism and Interracial Marriage." In *Interracial Marriage in Hawaii*. Edited by R. Adams. New York: Macmillan, 1937. Pp. 142–159.

Aldridge, Delores P.
1978 "Interracial Marriages: Empirical and Theoretical Considerations," *Journal of Black Studies*, 8(3):355–368. March.

America
1979 "For Better or Worse," America. P. 372. May 5.

Anson, Robert Sam
1982 "Black and White Together: Can Love Really Be Color-Blind?" *Ebony*. Pp. 146. August.

Argus, Carole
1984 "The Brides-to-Order Business," *Newsday*, Part II. Pp. 4–5. March 8.

Asian Week
1984 "UCLA Study Finds High Rate of Interracial Marriage among Nikkei," *Asian Week*. P. 3. November 10.

Baptiste, H. Prentice, Jr.
1983 "Rearing the Interracial Child." Paper Presented at Interracial Conference, New York.

Barnett, Larry
1963 "Interracial Marriage in California," *Marriage and Family Living*, 25:425–427. November.

Barron, Milton L.
1972 *The Blending American: Patterns of Intermarriage*. Chicago: Quadrangle Books.

——
1946 *People Who Intermarry*. Syracuse, NY: Syracuse University Press.

Bawden, Julie
1987a "Love Matches Across the Racial Barriers," *AsiAm*. Pp. 40–44. February.

1987b "Who's Afraid of Interracial Marriage?" *AsiAm.* Pp. 19–22, 76–77. February.

Bean, Frank D. and Linda H. Aiken
1976 "Intermarriage and Unwanted Fertility in the United States," *Journal of Marriage and the Family.* Pp. 61–72. February.

Belah, Robert *et al.*
1985 "Love and Marriage." In *Habits of the Heart.* Edited by Belah *et al.* New York: Harper & Row. Pp. 85–112.

Belkin, Lisa
1986 "The Mail-Order Marriage Business," *The New York Times Magazine.* Pp. 28–78. May 11.

Bennetts, Leslie
1979 "Interracial Couples Look at Life as Mixed Marriages Increase," *The New York Times.* P. A24. February 23.

Berman, Louis
1968 *Jews and Intermarriage.* New York: Thomas Yoseloff.

Besanceney, Paul H.
1965 "On Reporting Rates of Intermarriage," *American Journal of Sociology,* 70(6):717–721. May.

Biesanz, John and Luke M. Smith
1951 "Adjustment of Interethnic Marriages on the Isthmus of Panama," *American Sociological Review,* 16(6):814–822. December.

Bontemps, Alex
1975 "National Poll Reveals Startling New Attitudes on Intermarriage," *Ebony,* 30:144–151. September.

Brooks, Andree
1985 "Repeated Remarriage: A Growing Trend?" *The New York Times.* Pp. C1. February 27.

Burma, John H.
1963 "Interethnic Marriage in Los Angeles, 1948–1959," *Social Forces,* 42:156–165. December.

Cheng, C.K. and Douglas Yamamura
1957 "Interracial Marriage and Divorce in Hawaii," *Social Forces,* 36:77–84.

Chinatown News
1987 Vancouver. P. 8. February 3.

City Planning Commission
1986 "Asians in New York City." New York: City Planning Commission.

Cohen, Steven Martin
1980   *Interethnic Marriage and Friendship.* New York: Arno Press.

Collins, Glenn
1984   "Children of Interracial Marriage," *The New York Times.* P. C1. January 20.

——————
1985   "A New Look at Intermarriage in the U.S." *The New York Times.* P. C13. February 11.

Cretser, Gary A. and Joseph J. Leon
1982   "Intermarriage in the U.S.: An Overview of Theory and Research." In *Intermarriage in the United States.* New York: Haworth Press. Pp. 3–15.

Crohn, Joel
1986   "Ethnic Identity and Marital Conflict." New York: American Jewish Committee.

Crossette, Barbara
1987   "Melting is Slow in S.E. Asian Pot," *The New York Times.* P. E28. March 22.

East/West
1986   "Demography of Persons of Asian Descent," *East/West.* P. 9 October 9.

Eberhard, Mann and Jane Waldron
1977   "Intercultural Marriage and Child Rearing." In *Adjustment in Intercultural Marriage.* Edited by Wen Shing Tseng, *et al.* Honolulu: University of Hawaii Press.

Ebony
1982   "Black Women/White Men," *Ebony.* P. 78. August.

Endo, Russell and Dale Hirokawa
1983   "Japanese American Intermarriage." In *Free Inquiry in Creative Sociology,* 11(2):159–166. November.

Fitzpatrick, Joseph T. and Douglas T. Gurak
1979   "Hispanic Intermarriage in New York City: 1975." New York: Fordham University Hispanic Research Center.

Fong, Stanley
1973   "Assimilation and Changing Social Roles of Chinese Americans," *Journal of Social Issues,* 29(2):115–127.

Freedman, Maurice
1979   *The Study of Chinese Society.* Stanford: Stanford University Press.

Gardner, Robert, Bryant Robery and Peter Smith
1985   "Asian American Growth, Change, and Diversity." Washington, DC: Population Reference Bureau. October.

Glick, Clarence
1970   "Interracial Marriage and Admixture in Hawaii," *Social Biology,* 17(4):278–291. December.

Glick, Paul C.
1970 "Intermarriage among Ethnic Groups in the United States," *Social Biology,* 17(4):292–298. December.

Goldman, Ari L.
1987 "Two Faith Couples and Holiday Choices," *The New York Times.* P. B2. December 15.

Gordon, Milton
1964 *Assimilation in American Life.* New York: Oxford University Press. P. 116.

Gregory, James
1984 "Brides by Mail," *US.* Pp. 28–31. March 26.

Gunde, Patricia
1971 "Identity among Eurasians." Unpublished senior thesis, University of California, Berkeley. May.

Gurak, Douglas T. and Joseph P. Fitzpatrick
1982 "Intermarriage among Hispanic Ethnic Groups in New York City," *American Journal of Sociology,* 87(4):921–934.

_____
1978 "Intermarriage Patterns in the U.S.: Maximizing Information from the U.S. Census Public Use Samples," *Public Data Use,* 6(2):33–43. March.

Han Suyin
1965 *The Crippled Tree.* New York: G.P. Putnam.

Hartford Courant
1912 "Love Ended 1870 Test of Chinese School Here," *Hartford Courant.* March 26.

Hayano, David M.
1981 "Ethnic Identification and Disidentification: Japanese-American Views of Chinese-Americans," *Ethnic Groups,* 3:157–171.

Hill, May and Joyce Peltzer
1982 "A Report of Thirteen Groups for White Parents of Black Children," *Family Relations.* Pp. 557–565. October.

Ho, Man Keung
1984 *Building a Successful Intermarriage.* St. Meinrad, IN.: St. Meinrad Archabbey.

Hogben, Lancelot
1932 *Genetic Principles in Medicine and Social Science.* New York: Knopf.

Ikels, Charlotte
1985 "Parental Perspectives on the Significance of Marriage," *Journal of Marriage and the Family.* Pp. 253–264. May.

Jeter, Kris
1982 "Analytic Essay: Intercultural and Interracial Marriage." Edited by Gary Cretser and Joseph Leon. In *Intermarriage in the United States*. New York: Haworth Press. Pp. 105–111.

Jiobu, Robert M
1988 *Ethnicity and Assimilation*. Albany: State University of New York Press.

Kaihatsu, Jane B.
1985 "Interracial Marriage," *East/West*. P. 4 January 23.

Kennedy, Roby Jo
1944 "Single or Triple Melting Pot?" *American Journal of Sociology*, 49:331–339.

Kephart, William M.
1977 *The Family, Society, and Individual*, 4th edition. Boston: Houghton-Mifflin.

Kich, George Kitahara
1982 *Eurasians: Ethnic/Racial Identity: Development of Bi-Japanese/White Adults*. Berkeley, CA: Wright Institute, Ph.D. Dissertation.

Kim, Elaine
1982 *Asian American Literature*. Philadelphia: Temple University Press.

Kitano, Harry
1961 "Differential Child-Rearing Attitudes Between First and Second Generation Japanese in the United States," *Journal of Social Psychology*, 53:13–19.

Kitano, H. and Lynn Kyung Chai
1982 "Korean Interracial Marriage." In *Intermarriage in the United States*. Edited by Gary Cretser and Joseph Leon. New York: Haworth Press. Pp. 75–89.

Kitano, H and Wai-Tsang Yeung
1982 "Chinese Interracial Marriage." In *Intermarriage in the United States*. Edited by Gary Cretser and Joseph Leon. New York: Haworth Press. Pp. 35–48.

Kitano, H., Wai-Tsang Yeung, Lynn Chai and Herbert Hatanaka
1984 "Asian American Interracial Marriage," *Journal of Marriage and the Family*, 46:179–190. February.

Krich, John
1986 "Here Come the Brides," *Mother Jones*. Pp. 34–46. February/March.

Lee, Bill Lann
1971 "Yung Wing and the Americanization of China," *Amerasia Journal*, 1(1):25–32. March.

Lee, Che-Fu, Raymond H. Potvin and Mary Verdieck
1974 "Interethnic Marriage as an Index of Assimilation: The Case of Singapore," *Social Forces*, 53(1):112–119. September.

Lee, Cherylene
1986 "Asian Men and Women: Why No Match?" *East/West*. P. 5. July 31.

Leonetti, Donna Lockwood and Laura Newell-Morris
1982 "Exogamy and Change in the Biosocial Structure of a Modern Urban Population," *American Anthropologist*, 84: 19–36.

Lind, Andrew W.
1967 *Hawaii's People*. Honolulu: University of Hawaii Press. Pp. 107–112.

———
1964 "Interracial Marriage as Affecting Divorce in Hawaii," *Sociology and Social Research*, 49:17–26.

Loewen, James
1971 *The Mississippi Chinese: Between Black and White*. Cambridge: Harvard University Press.

Markoff, Richard
1977 "Intercultural Marriage: Problem Areas." In *Adjustment in Intercultural Marriage*. Edited by Wen-Shing Tseng, *et al*. Honolulu: University of Hawaii Press.

Mayer, Egon
1985 *Love and Tradition: Marriage Between Jews and Christians*. New York: Plenum Press.

———
1978 "Patterns of Intermarriage among American Jews: Varieties, Uniformities, Dilemmas, and Prospects." American Jewish Committee.

Mayer, Egon and Carl Sheingold
1979 "Intermarriage and the Jewish Future." American Jewish Committee.

Mayer, John E.
1980 *Jewish-Gentile Courtships*. Westport, CT: Greenwood Press.

McCunn, Ruthanne Lum
1981 *Thousand Pieces of Gold*. San Francisco: Design Enterprises.

Merton, Robert
1941 "Intermarriage and Social Structure: Fact and Theory," *Psychiatry*, 4:361–374. August.

Miller, Michael H.
1971 "Comparison of the Duration of Interracial with Intraracial Marriages in Hawaii," *International Journal of Sociology of the Family*, 1(2):1–5. September.

Mittelbach, Frank, Joan W. Moore and Ronald McDaniel
1966 "Intermarriage of Mexican Americans." Mexican American Study Project Advance Report No. 6. Los Angeles: University of California, Los Angeles. November.

Monahan, Thomas
1979a "Interracial Marriage and Divorce in Kansas and the Question of Instability of Mixed Marriages," In *Cross-Cultural Perspectives of Mate-Selection and Marriage*. Edited by George Kurian. Westport, CT.: Greenwood Press. Pp. 350–363.

———
1979b "Interracial Marriage in a Southern Area: Maryland, Virginia, and the District of Columbia." In *Cross-Cultural Perspectives of Mate-Selection and Marriage*. Edited by George Kurian. Westport, CT. Greenwood Press. Pp. 287–311.

———
1976 "Overview of Statistics on Interracial Marriage in the United States, with Data on its Extent from 1963–1970," *Journal of Marriage and the Family*, 38:223–331. May.

———
1970 "Are Interracial Marriages Really Less Stable?" *Social Forces*, 48:461–473. June.

Morton, Newton, Chin S. Chung and Ming-Pi Mi
1967 *Genetics of Interracial Crosses in Hawaii*. Basel, Switzerland: S. Karger.

Muntzing, Arne
1961 *Genetics: Basic and Applied*. Stockholm: Lts. Forlag.

Murphy-Shigematsu, Stephen
1987 "Voices of Amerasians: Ethnicity, Identity and Empowerment in Interracial Japanese Americans" Unpublished Doctoral dissertation, Harvard University.

Murray, Pauli, comp.
1950 *States' Laws on Race and Color*. Cincinnati: Women's Division of Christian Service, Board of Missions of the Methodist Church Service Center. Also Supplement, 1955.

Nakashima, Cynthia
1987 "Research Notes on Nikkei Hapa Identity." Paper presented at Asian American Studies Conference, Santa Clara University.

Newsweek
1987 "Portrait of Divorce in America," *Newsweek*. P. 78 February 2.

———
1986 "Too Late for Prince Charming?" *Newsweek*. Pp. 53–61. June 2.

———
1984 "Children of the Rainbow," *Newsweek*. Pp. 121–122. November 19.

Norton, Arthur J. and Jeanne E. Moorman
1987 "Current Trends in Marriage and Divorce among American Women", *Journal of Marriage and the Family*, 49:3–14. February.

Palmer, Sally
1979 "Reasons for Marriage Breakdown: A Case Study in Southwestern Ontario Canada," In *Cross Cultural Perspectives of Mate-Selection and Marriage*. Edited by George Kurian. Westport, CT: Greenwood Press. Pp. 364–375.

Petschek, William
1985 "Outreach Programs to Intermarried Couples." New York American Jewish Committee.

Planas, Alvan and Diana Chow, eds.
1978 *Winter Blossoms*. Berkeley: University of California, Asian American Studies Department.

Porterfield, Ernest
1978 *Black and White Mixed Marriages*. Chicago: Nelson Hall.

Ratliff, Bascom W., Harriett Faye Moon and Gwendolyn A. Bonnaci
1978 "Intercultural Marriage: The Korean American Experience," *Social Casework,* 59:221–226. April.

Schewertfeger, Margaret M.
1982 "Interethnic Marriage and Divorce in Hawaii: A Panel Study of 1968 First Marriages." In *Intermarriage in the United States*. New York: Haworth Press. Pp. 49–59.

Schwartz, S.
1951 "Mate Selection among New York City's Chinese Males, 1931–1938," *American Journal of Sociology,* 56:562–568. May.

Shorter, Edward
1975 *The Making of the Modern Family*. New York: Basic Books.

Spickard, Paul R.
1989 *Mixed Blood*. Madison: University of Wisconsin Press.

Spivey, Philip
1984 "Positive Approaches to Self-Identity in Children of Interracial Unions." Panel discussion at Conference by Council on Interracial Books for Children, June 15–16.

Strauss, Anselm
1972 "Strain and Harmony in American Japanese War-Bride Marriages." In *The Blending American*. Edited by Milton Barron. Chicago: Quadrangle Books. Pp. 268–281.

Sui Sin Far (Edith Eaton)
1987 "Leaves from the Mental Portfolio of an Eurasian," *Chinese American History and Perspectives, 1987*. San Francisco: Chinese Historical Society. Pp. 169–183.

Sung, Betty Lee
1987   *The Adjustment Experience of Chinese Immigrant Children in New York City.* Staten Island: Center for Migration Studies.

‾‾‾‾‾
1987   "Intermarriage among the Chinese in New York City." In *Chinese America: History and Perspective 1987.* San Francisco: Chinese Historical Society. Pp. 101–118.

‾‾‾‾‾
1967   *Mountain of Gold.* New York: Macmillan.

Tachiki, Amy *et al.*, eds.
1970   "White Male Qualities." In *Roots: An Asian American Reader.* Edited by Amy Tachiki, *et al.* Los Angeles, University of California Los Angeles, Asian American Studies Center. Pp. 44–45. (Reprinted from *Gidra*, January 1970).

Takaki, Ronald
1989   *Strangers from a Different Shore.* Boston: Little Brown and Company.

Tanaka, Ron
1971   "I Hate My Wife for Her Flat Yellow Face." In *Roots: An Asian American Reader.* Edited by Amy Tachiki *et al.* 1971. Los Angeles: University of California Asian American Studies Center. P. 47. (Reprinted from *Gidra*, 1969).

Tinker, John N.
1982   "Intermarriage and Assimilation in a Plural Society," In *Intermarriage in the United States.* New York: Haworth Press. Pp. 61–74.

‾‾‾‾‾
1973   "Intermarriage and Ethnic Boundaries: The Japanese American Case," *Journal of Social Issues,* 29(2):49–66.

Toland, John
1985   *Gods of War.* New York: Doubleday.

Tseng, Wen-shing, John McDermott and Thomas Maretzki
1977   *Adjustment in Intercultural Marriage.* Honolulu: University of Hawaii Press.

Unger, Michael
1984   "When Breaking Up Beats Making Up," *Newsday.* P. 3. October 16.

U.S. Immigration and Naturalization Service.
        Annual *Statistical Yearbooks.*

U.S. News and World Report
1983   "Marriage is Back in Style," *U.S. News and World Report.* Pp. 44–50.

Washington Post
1985   "Immigrants Subdue Divorce Rate," *Washington Post.* Pp. 1 and 6. December.

Weiss, Melford S.
1969   "Inter-racial Romance: The Chinese-Caucasian Dating Game." Paper presented at S.W. Anthropological Association Conference.

"White Male Qualities," *Gidra.* p. 85.

Wilson, Anne
1984   "Mixed Race Children in British Society: Some Theoretical Considerations," *British Journal of Sociology,* 35(1):42–61.

Wilson, Barbara Foley
1984   "Marriages Melting Pot," *American Demographics,* 6 (7):34–38.

Wood, Margaret Mary
1934   *The Stranger.* New York: Columbia University Press.

Yuan, D.Y.
1980   "Significant Demographic Characteristics of Chinese Who Intermarry in the United States," *California Sociologist,* 3(2):184–196. Summer.

Yung Wing
1909   *My Life in China and America.* New York: Henry Holt.

Index